UNSUNG HEROES
Black History 2021

"For many are called, but few are chosen."
Matthew 22:14 KJV

This book is dedicated to all past, present, and future fighters of systematic oppression. It is also dedicated to my amazing mother, Mrs. Cassandra McBride-Nash for all of the sacrifices you made for us. I love you mom.

Dr. Mary McBride-Brown

 **Black History: We've come a long way!**

Martin, Harriet, Cicely, and John
Just look at how far we have come.
On the backs of those who toiled.
Fingers clenched in dirt and soil.

Don't stop now; there's much to do.
I'm creating a path for you to go through.
Lifting my dirty hands to fix your crown.
No intentions of pulling or tearing you down.

A blessed transformation from then to now.
And God keeps making ways somehow.
They can't come for you, without coming for me.
Our victory is our legacy.

—— MARY BROWN
DAILY INSPIRATION

I appeal to you, brothers, by the name of our Lord Jesus Christ, that all of you agree, and that there be no divisions among you, but that you be united in the same mind and the same judgment.
1 Corinthians 1:10 ESV

Dark Emotions: Honoring History, Creating Legacy: Black History 2021

Copyright © 2021 by **Dr. Mary McBride-Brown**. All rights reserved. No part of this book may be reproduced or transmitted in any form or by any means without written permission from the author Dr. Mary McBride-Brown.

ISBN: **9798707301186**

Fishing Lessons
By: Dr. Mary McBride-Brown

The tasks may be challenging, but you can do it!
You CAN accomplish new things and go far!
Don't fall into the trap of being pacified.
They aren't favoring you by lowering the bar.

Just because it looks hard doesn't mean it's impossible.
Go ahead and prove yourself right.
Don't allow their cursed speech to label you.
Stand tall, work hard, and stay in the fight.

People will make you think it's what's best for you,
By giving you boatloads of fish.
If they really cared to see a better you,
They would teach you how to fish.

Know Better! Do Better! Be Better!

Therefore encourage one another and build one another up, just as you are doing. 1 Thessalonians 5:11 ESV

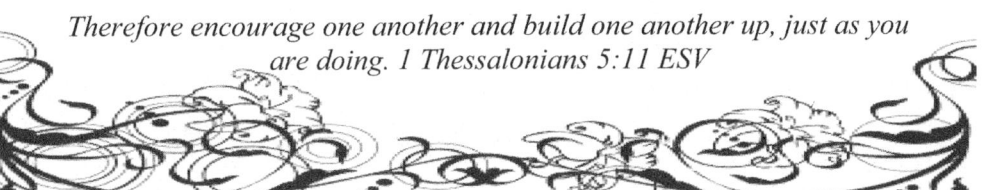

Dark Emotions

CONTENTS

Fishing Lessons
Honoring History

DR. MARY MCBRIDE-BROWN
Visions of the Past
Dear Heavenly Father
9

HALEIGH MCGEE
11

TYREE DAVIS
12

MURIEL SIMMONS
15

DR. MARY MCBRIDE-BROWN
Visions of the Hoodies
Dear Heavenly Father
18

LEM E. MCBRIDE
20

DR. MARY MCBRIDE-BROWN
Visions of the NFL
Dear Heavenly Father
24

JAMARION ADDISON
26

KWATRIVIOUS JOHNSON
28

TYLER GLASS
31

BOOKER CHAMBERS
33

DR. MARY MCBRIDE-BROWN
Visions of the Present
Dear Heavenly Father
35

AISHA ERMA LENORA SAFFOLD
37

TROY BROWN, JR.
BETA RHO CHAPTER OF OMEGA PSI PHI
41

JERVIS MCGEE
45

DR. CHRISTINA A.R. GLADNEY
48

LATRICE SMITH
53

NIEMA JONES-STRONG
56

DENISE PITCHFORD
59

TOPAZ THORTON
62

DERANDIUS SIMMONS, SR.
66

CLINTON GATEWOOD
69

Dark Emotions

LULA ELLIS
72

PATRICIA YOUNG
74

LINDA PAYNE
76

MIKE GUINN
78

FREDDIE WHITE-JOHNSON
80

SYLVIA CLARK
88

PASTOR MARILYN JONES
91

DR. MARY MCBRIDE-BROWN
Visions of the Future
Dear Heavenly Father
93

JOANN BUFORD
95

MIRANDA HODGE
97

BARBARA GRAY
105

DR. MARY NASH ROBINSON
108

REV. JESSIE PAYNE, JR.
112

Dark Emotions

THELMA COLLINS
114

DEVON DENISE YORK
118

DR. MARY MCBRIDE-BROWN
120
Creating Legacy
Black Girl Transformation
My Ph.D.
Teach Me to Fish
Quietly Unbothered
Daily Inspirations

BLACK HISTORY QUESTIONS: SURVEY RESULTS
130

About the Author
168

HONORING HISTORY

To date, I have published seven books, and all of them caused me to shed a few tears. Why? Because I refuse to invest my time as an author in creating books that lack the purpose of empowering and inspiring young and older people. I also refuse to stop trying to provide People of Color with factual information that will allow them to free themselves and their families of every depressive and deceptive generational curse that keeps them disillusioned and operating in fear. Will my efforts ever be successful? We will see.

I believe it would be factual to say that every Person of Color is grateful for the many self-sacrificing works and hardships faced by our ancestors who braved the long-lasting persecutions, executions, and assassinations of their characters, dignities, and freedoms as they fought to make our lives better. I could list many of their names and still wouldn't have enough energy in my fingers to type them all. However, we are still grateful.

So why did I not just write a book about our heroes of the past? I didn't write about them because their stories will forever be engrained in our souls. Their works will forever exude through the pores of our skin. To be clear, we are a result of their actions and pains.

This book highlights only a few of the many of those carrying on our ancestors' legacies who risked their lives to help set us free. **Are we free? My answer is no,** but we have a lot more luxuries than those who endured sufferings to make us free. And although the freedom fighters of the past may not be here to see how far their efforts have come, I'm sure in some cases, they are all proud of us. In other cases, I'm also certain they are disappointed in our silence and inability to unify as a whole. But for now, let us all rejoice as we honor our history by featuring their legacies.

Visions of the Past
By: Dr. Mary McBride-Brown

I saw a brown man hanging there.
Head bowed, feet dangling in the air.
No wish, no wind could pull him down.
They stood, they laughed, pointing from the ground.

I saw a dark girl running towards the woods,
Their arms stretched out to steal her goods.
Heartbeats, I heard, pounding miles away.
Her lifeless body found in the noonday.

I saw bronzed people sitting in the pews.
Trusting and believing one day for good news.
Praying that someday life wouldn't be so hard.
With every passing day, they kept faith in God.

Dear Heavenly Father,

We come to you asking for divine grace, mercy, and favor over the lives of these young people. Bless them as they work to be a blessing to others through their ***positive actions and talents***. Let no weapon formed against them prosper. Cover their young ears and eyes so that they are protected from the negative stares and discouraging comments of this world regarding their efforts. Block every deceptive spirit sent against them. Use your holy angels to watch over them day and night. Bless every good thing that their precious hands touch.

We decree and declare your divine favor, peace, wisdom, understanding, love, and prosperity over their lives.

In the name of Christ Jesus, we pray. Amen.

HALEIGH MCGEE
Age 6
Itta Bena, MS
(Rapper, YouTube Personality, Entertainer)

Haleigh McGee is a 6-year-old *"straight-A student."* Her ambitions and talents far exceed anyone's expectations of a young child. She is an extremely talented **upcoming rapper, YouTube personality, and entertainer**.

Haleigh goes above and beyond to make her family proud. Each day she continues to amaze everyone she meets. She is destined for greatness because she knows how to apply herself with the tools God gave her. Her hobbies are making slime, creating TikToks, and rapping. She is a very bright and intelligent young girl who is on the horizon of becoming a star.

"As a father, I will try my best to coach her to reach her full potential. As long as she is making good grades in school, I am fine with her engaging in other activities." says her dad Jervis.

TYREE DAVIS
Age 14
Itta Bena, MS
(Published Author, Motivational Speaker)
Over 40,000 Books Sold

Tyree Deshawn Davis is an African American author who began making vivid stories when he was the delicate age of three years old. His older sister would be the teacher, and Tyree would pose as the willing student. When Tyree began writing at the age of four, he scribbled and told stories to go along with his scribbles. Tyree's mother knew that he would have the family's gift of writing as she listened to him describe characters and events that were not shown on any of his scribbled filled pages.

Tyree became a published author for the first time in 2013. He wrote a book entitled *"The Wonderful Adventures of Rufus & Burtha, The Possums."* This main character, Rufus was based on a real-life character in Tyree's immediate family, his brother Kingston, who had been diagnosed with Autism.

Along with his mother Brandy, Tyree was able to put his imagination on paper and stir the souls of thousands around the world, so much so that he was asked to be featured on a few nationally syndicated shows like *Good Morning America* and *BET's 106th & Park*; thus, selling over 40,000 copies of his book.

To date, Tyree has served as a speaker at many children's forums for writing. He has been awarded numerous awards for spoken word poetry and has shared his love for reading and writing by hosting reading segments at local libraries.

Tyree has written one book and over 60 poems and short stories. Tyree is currently working on a book series entitled *"The Junior High Chronicles: The Underground School House."* He is inspired by children who have special needs and their will to yet be great despite challenges beyond their control. This inspiration stems from Tyree's deep love and respect for his brother Kingston who has Autism.

Tyree's future aspiration is to attend a HBCU, major in Communications, and become a traveling activist for children with special needs. His motto in life is, *"Every day Is A New Opportunity to Grow Taller, To Reach Farther, To Catch The "Me's" of Yesterday."*

Dark Emotions

MURIEL SIMMONS
Age: 15
Memphis, TN
(CEO of Muriel's Creation, Entrepreneur, Fashionista)

I, Muriel Simmons, am 15 years old. I am the daughter of Derandius and Sabrevian Simmons. I am the oldest of a twin sister Madison Simmons. I am a 10th grader at PowerCenter Academy High School in Memphis, TN.

In 2020, I decided to start my own business "Muriel's Creation." In doing this, I also decided to enroll in a program at the Academy of Arts to get a jump start on my career path as a Fashion Designer. I enrolled in the Summer program and started taking classes to learn more about the journey I would be soon embarking on as a designer. I am also a member of my school's Rugby team. I enjoy singing and spending time with my family.

Who are your most significant influences?
Up to this point in my life, my influences have been my past teachers. When I was in the first grade attending elementary school, my first-grade teacher, Mrs. Anderson, would tell me I needed to stay in the first grade because I wasn't as great of a reader as the other students in the class. My third-grade teacher Mrs. Shaw-Hill would tell me I would never amount to anything because I wasn't learning at the pace of the other students or reading as well. Some may see their statements as being horrible or just mean. I viewed their words differently and wanted to prove them wrong. Once I got to middle school, ALL of my teachers were more encouraging and supportive, which helped me improve and achieve academic levels that others said I couldn't reach.

What are your future goals?
My goal in life is to make myself proud. What I mean about this is I need to do what makes me happy. My goal is to get up every day and enjoy life and all it has to offer. My career goal is to be a Fashion Designer. I plan to attend the Academy of Arts University in San Francisco, CA. I plan to earn a Business Degree as well and learn how to market.

What do you attribute to your success?
My passion/love of fashion has contributed to the start of my business "Muriel's Creation: The support from my family has helped me establish a business as well as learn how to become a responsible person.

What advice would you give to other young people?
My advice I would give to youth is that it is okay to DREAM BIG. Always strive to go higher and never allow anyone to make you feel or believe your dreams are not REACHABLE.

What your favorite quote?
My favorite quotes are:
"Beauty is within and not out."
"Fashion is not a Style; it is a VOICE."

What are you doing to bring awareness and spark change?
Some of the things I have done to bring awareness and spark change was to be no longer silent about my feelings and emotions. I now share and am more vocal in conversations with young girls like me.

I've also shared my experiences with the non-profit organization called Youth Villages. In 2020, I was inducted into the VIP program at my school, PowerCenter Academy High. In this group, an individual has to meet specific qualifications, including 95% attendance, 3.5 GPA or higher, and meet NWEA (MAP) standards.

Why have you committed to your cause(s)?
I am committed to making a difference in other people's lives because I have experienced firsthand what it feels like to be unaccepted or put down. The world is so chaotic and lacks unity and peace that if my generation or peers can see someone like them do positive things, it can allow them to think differently and dream big.

Visions of Hoodies
By: Dr. Mary McBride-Brown

I used to buy you everything,
You needed for your covering.
But now I shudder all the more,
When you put on your hoodie and exit my door.

Who would have thought that such a shirt,
Could cause so many families to hurt?
Because someone feels justified,
To profile your hoodie like the FBI.

So, for the days you put it on,
I anoint your head and charge my phone.
Praying all through the day you'll return home to me,
Without someone attacking your hoodie.

Dark Emotions

Dear Heavenly Father,

We come to you asking for divine grace, mercy, and favor over the lives of our young people who are ***victims of racial profiling***.
We ask that you protect our young Black men who aren't able to safely jog down a street, wear a hoodie, walk in a store, or even ride in a nice vehicle without being unfairly targeted and harassed by those who have low self-esteem.
Let no weapon formed against them prosper. Let every tongue that rises against them be condemned. The plans of the enemy against them are destroyed.
Block every lying, underhanded, and deceptive spirit sent against them. Erase the stigma placed on their hoodies. Let your holy angels watch over them day and night.
Bless every good thing that their precious hands touch.
We decree and declare your divine favor, peace, wisdom, understanding, love, and prosperity over their lives.

In the name of Christ Jesus, we pray. Amen.

LEM E. MCBRIDE
Age 18
Grenada, MS
(Future Book Publisher, Published Co-Author,
Graduating High School Senior, Future Nurse/Veterinarian)

"I am not my hoodie."

Lem McBride is a 12th-grade student at Grenada High School. He is a member of the Grenada High School's marching band, the symphonic band, and jazz band. Lem has participated in Honor Band opportunities, such as the Stately Oaks Honor's Band at Louisiana State University and The University of Mississippi's Honor Band.

Lem ultimately aspires to become a veterinarian. He enjoys taking care of his family's five horses and five German Shepherds. He has always been an animal lover. He plans to enroll at a university to pursue a degree in nursing in the Fall of 2021. His goal is to earn and use his degree to continue funding his education as he continues his studies to obtain a Doctor of Veterinary Medicine.

Lem is also working with his mom, who has now published seven books. He assists with book cover designing, word placement, and picture formatting. He plans to continue working to help get his mom's book publishing business established. Lem has also been a co-author of two anthologies.

Who are your most significant influences?
My dad and mom will always be my greatest influences. They have always supported me and made sure I had many opportunities to be included in activities.

As a young Black man, my dad, Regis, Sr., has always been my biggest role model. I have always been able to talk to him about everything. I appreciate him for always being present and active in my life. I don't think I would be the person I am today without his love and support.

My other most significant influences are many of the males in my family.

My brother Regis, Jr. has always been an influential person for me. He is my only sibling. He is a go-getter. I appreciate the advice he gives me. He has always set a positive example for me.

My Uncle Lem, Jr. is definitely a positive role model for me. I admire him because not only is he a responsible family man, but also has served in the military for all of my life. He also reminds me of my dad by how he cares for and interacts with his sons (my cousins).

I also have been influenced by those in the media, such as Denzel Washington, Morgan Freeman, Kevin Edwards, Jr., and J. Cole. Those in the media do have an impact on others, especially young people like me. We just have to choose good role models.

What are your future goals?
Like any person, I want to be wealthy. I want to take care of my family. In order to get there, I plan to continue helping my mother with her book publishing company. I also plan to enroll in college and major in Nursing. Yes. I am going to be a male nurse. I want to go to school to become a veterinarian eventually, but I'm going to work at reaching my goals in stages for now.

What do you attribute to your success?
My dad and mom are the reason I am who I am today. They both pushed and helped prepare me to be successful.

What advice would you give to other young people?
Open your minds and learn to think deeper about things. Success comes to those who push to get it. Push harder.

What are your favorite quotes?
"There's no such thing as a life that's better than yours."
"For what's money without happiness? Or hard times without the people you love?"
"I might bend a little bit, but I don't fold."
-J. Cole

What are you doing to bring awareness and spark change?
I want to serve as a positive role model to show Black teens and young men that they can be positive, have fun, and still achieve. With a positive mindset, and a desire to do better, we can move ourselves to the next level.

Dark Emotions

Why have you committed to your cause(s)?
I believe that just looking at the state we live in (Mississippi) while being Black makes many of us feel depressed. One day, if we work together, we could rebuild our communities and the side of towns where the majority of the Blacks live. I want our side of towns to be just as pleasant as the areas not heavily populated by Blacks.

Visions of the NFL
By: Dr. Mary McBride-Brown

You are more than just jerseys and tights.
I admire your drive. I see your fight.
All you ever wanted was a chance,
To show the world you can advance.

Stay on that field and do your thing.
One day you will achieve your dream,
Of entering the National Football League,
Where all of the world will be intrigued.

But while you wait for everyone to see,
Work hard in school and earn your degree.
There are many of us rooting for you,
Because you're doing the things, you said you could do.

Keep praying! Stay humble! Your future is bright.
You've made it this far. Don't give up the fight.
And as you go higher, just keep standing tall.
And never forget who passed you the ball.

Dear Heavenly Father,

We come to you asking for divine grace, mercy, and favor over the lives of our young people who are *shaking off labels.*
We ask that you protect our young Black athletes who have to work ten times as hard to be recognized over those who have mediocre talents yet inherit favoritism.

Let no weapon formed against them prosper. Let every tongue that rises against them be condemned. The plans of the enemy against them are destroyed.
Block every lying, underhanded, and deceptive spirit sent against them. Erase the stigma placed on their intellect.

Let your holy angels watch over them day and night. Bless every good thing that their precious hands touch.
We decree and declare your divine favor, peace, wisdom, understanding, love, and prosperity over their lives.

In the name of Christ Jesus, we pray. Amen.

JAMARION ADDISON
Age 19
Greenwood, MS
(College Student, Future Business Administrator/Accountant)

Born in Milwaukee, WI, Jamarion Addison is now a star athlete at Navarro College in Dallas, Texas. During his junior year of high school, Jamarion relocated to Greenwood, MS.

He wants to follow in the footsteps of his father, who was also played football. Jamarion serves as a positive, young, African American role model for young Black males aspiring to obtain a college degree and success in athletics.

Who are your greatest influences?

My dad is my greatest influence. He has always been a positive role model for me, and I want to do everything I can to make him proud.

What are your future goals?

I hope to continue playing football in college while working on my Master's degree in Business Administration or Accounting.

What do you attribute to your success?

Losing close family members motivated and pushed me to aim higher and work harder to reach my goals. I am also grateful for the close family members who continued to encourage me to succeed.

What advice would you give to other young people?

Don't ever let anyone tell you what you cannot do. You can do anything you make up your mind to do.

What your favorite quote?

"When you want to succeed as bad as you want to breathe, then you will be successful." -Eric Thomas

KWATRIVOUS JOHNSON
AKA
"DOLLAR BILL"
Age 21
Greenwood, MS
(College Student, Future NFL Player,
Future Sports Psychologist)

Kwatrivious "Dollar Bill" Johnson is a star athlete at Mississippi State University. He is also being sought after by National Football League (NFL) scouts and teams. He serves as a positive, young, African American role model for young Black males aspiring to succeed in athletics. Not only is "Dollar Bill" dominating the football field, but he is also excelling in his studies at MSU.

Who are your greatest influences?

I am always inspired by my dad, mom, and grandmother. They all are sources of strength for me. They have always been supportive of me and my dreams. I thank them for always believing in me.

One of my most significant influences is Coach Clinton Gatewood. Along with my dad, mom, and grandmother, he is a major reason why I played and continue to play football. There were many times I wanted to quit, but Coach Gatewood pushed me to keep going. He and my family always encouraged me never to give up.

What are your future goals?

I want to be drafted into the NFL. I also want to earn my degree and become a sports psychologist. After my NFL career, I want to use my degree in the field I enjoy. I also want to remain active and an activist in my community. I want to see my community thrive. I want to serve as a positive role model for other young people.

What do you attribute to your success?

I've made it this far because I have a great support system. I am incredibly blessed and lucky to have supportive people in my life. My support system always made sure I remained focused. They kept me on track and made sure I avoided the streets. They demanded that I always be respectful. I was always encouraged to show up to places, classes, and appointments on time. I was always told to do everything to the best of my ability.

What advice would you give to other young people?

Believe in God and give Him praise. Your dreams will come true if you work hard and believe. Keep grinding even when things are not working in your favor. If you love what you're doing, keep doing it to the best of your ability. Your hard work and efforts will pay off.

My mom used to tell me all of the time to *"EAT."* It meant that I needed to keep grinding, keep working, and never give up. I offer this advice to everyone else. I'm glad to be a role model for others. It is an honor and privilege that I don't take lightly. I want young

Black males to know that dreams do come true to those who keep grinding.

TYLER GLASS
Age 22
Greenwood, MS
(College Student, Future NFL Player & Football Coach)

Tyler Glass is currently pursuing his dream of becoming a professional football player. He is working hard to earn his degree at the University of Louisiana Monroe. He serves as a positive, young, African American role model for young Black males aspiring to obtain a college degree and success in athletics.

Who are your greatest influences?
My parents are my greatest influences. It is because of them that I am able to continue to chase my dreams. They have always supported my interests and pushed me to do my best. I would not have made it this far without them.

Coach Antoine Williams is another person who inspired me at a young age. As I got older, I met Coach Clinton Gatewood. Both he and Mr. Williams inspire me because they carry themselves as real men in my eyes. They don't mind helping other young men and encouraging us all to stay out of trouble. They have always stressed the importance of us (young Black males) doing better.

What are your future goals?
I know my future is promising. I want to play in the NFL and also become a football coach. I want to train individuals with the same dedication, passion, and concern I received from those who coached me, especially Coach Williams & Coach Gatewood.

What do you attribute to your success?
I have always remained focused, humbled, and never backed down from any task or challenge.

What advice would you give to other young people?
Always stay humble and hungry. If you believe you can do it, you can do it!

What your favorite quote?
"Never look back. Always look forward. Never give up."
-Tyler Glass

BOOKER T. CHAMBERS
Age 23
Greenwood, MS
(College Graduate, College Football Standout, Future Football Head Coach)

Booker T. Chambers is no stranger to the spotlight. He is most notable for his speed and fancy footwork on the football field. He serves as a positive, young, African American role model for young Black males aspiring to obtain a college degree and success in athletics.

Who are your greatest influences?
The greatest influences in my life are my parents. The inspired me to be the man I am today. My parents are both brilliant, smart,

and driven. I could not have made it without them. They inspired me to play sports and play well.

What are your future goals?
I know God didn't bring me this far for me not to accomplish all of my goals. I have successfully earned my bachelor's degree. I still hope to become a head football coach and establish my own youth sports organization.

What do you attribute to your success?
God, faith, and self-determination are all the reasons I have made it this far.

What advice would you give to other young people?
Life is pretty much what you make of it. Never give up on your goals and dreams. Always have a back-up plan.

What your favorite quote?
"Be legendary. No matter what you do, leave a legendary legacy."
-Booker T. Chambers

Visions of the Present
By: Dr. Mary McBride-Brown

A brown-skinned man opened up the doors,
For his brown-skinned girls to walk the floors.
A new tone was set by his brown-skin spouse
As they welcomed us into the White House.

A brown-skinned woman nearly stole the show.
As her name was called to stand alongside Joe.
Such a sight to behold as never before.
History made once again on the White House floor.

Here you are still standing through thick and thin.
Hoping to open up more doors for women and men.
Yes, it's hard but just keep striving and soon you will see
It's your time to make the world better for you and me.

Dear Heavenly Father,

We come to you asking for divine grace, mercy, and favor over the lives of our ***present history makers.***
We ask that you protect our young Black gamechangers who are thinking outside of the box and pushing us out of our comfort zones.

Let no weapon formed against them prosper. Let every tongue that rises against them be condemned. The plans of the enemy against them are destroyed.
Block every lying, underhanded, and deceptive spirit sent against them. Erase the stigma placed on their motives.

Let your holy angels watch over them day and night. Bless every good thing that their precious hands touch.
We decree and declare your divine favor, peace, wisdom, understanding, love, and prosperity over their lives.

In the name of Christ Jesus, we pray. Amen.

Dark Emotions

AISHA ERMA LENORA SAFFOLD
Age 28
Lexington, MS
(Founder and Executive Director of P.E.A.R.L.S. Mentoring for Girls Inc.)

A pearl begins as a particle of dust or dirt that finds its way inside an oyster. Then, the oyster coats the particle repeatedly over time-- up to two to four years -- until the finished product is a smooth, lustrous white pearl, which often has a value the same as a gemstone, ranging from hundreds to even millions of dollars.

They're found at the bottom of the ocean. They take all the grime and the dust and the dirt from the sea, and they form this valuable gem. *For Aisha Erma Lenora Saffold, she takes the girl's issues with self-esteem, insecurities, worries, and all the negativity they may have about themselves, and molds it into a P.E.A.R.L.S. girl.*

Dark Emotions

Aisha Erma Lenora Saffold is the Founder and Executive Director of P.E.A.R.L.S. Mentoring for Girls Inc., a 501(c)3 nonprofit organization where they are striving to "Change Lives, One PEARL at a Time in the State of Mississippi.

Born to a retired principal and Mississippi cattle farmer and welder, her parents instilled in her, at a young age, the importance of being a servant and having a servant's spirit. To her, that meant being a blessing to others as we have been blessed. This teaching is the core foundation of the mentoring program she founded in December 2015.

She is from a small Mississippi town in Holmes County known as Lexington, MS. It's one of the United States' most impoverished counties, with more than 33% of the population living in poverty. Lexington lacks many resources, which then results in harmful exposure.

More than 1 in 4 children in the rural South and nearly as many women live in poverty. When race and ethnicity are considered, the poverty rate is more than double for African-Americans girls. Because of this, P.E.A.R.L.S. continues to instill in our Mississippi girls, "It's not where you come from, but where you're going."

She started P.E.A.R.L.S. because of a need to clean up all those stains that others have marked on ones and us and the ones we have placed on ourselves. Aisha believes that every girl, no matter where she comes from, deserves to fulfill her utmost potential. Because of this, she strives to mold our girls into role models, powerful women who achieve their hopes and dreams.

Our P.E.A.R.L.S. members are led by young women who serve as mentors, and in turn, our mentors develop leadership skills that they will carry with them throughout life. We strive to help young teenage girls build self-esteem, develop leadership skills, and recognize community importance.

She aspires to empower young women to believe in themselves

and teach them that validation comes from oneself. In a society where the media implants a false image of whom and what a young woman should resemble, she has vowed to take a stand to teach the contrary and impart knowledge and wisdom in PEARL's lives. **She wants every Mississippi girl to know that they are intelligent and beautiful and can reach their goals and excel at all they put their hands towards doing.** As long as they have someone in their corner backing and pushing them to pursue their dreams, they will attain them.

She wants all of the world to know that good people and good things are happening in the Great State of Mississippi.

Aisha knows that our Mississippi girls are future presidents, C.E.O.'s, ambassadors, producers, doctors, teachers, entrepreneurs, and molding and shaping them; they can achieve so much more.

Why have you committed to your cause(s)?
I decided to commit to this cause of mentoring the lives of our Mississippi girls because if not us, then who? If not now, when? We talk about the problems, but what are we doing to fix them?

What would you like to see happen as a result of what you are doing?
I would like to see the girls who come through our program go off and do wonderful, life-changing, and groundbreaking things. That magic won't only spread to everyone in their surroundings but showcase Mississippi but, most importantly, the Mississippi Delta in a positive light.

What is your favorite quote?
My favorite quote is, *"We are blessed so that we could be a blessing to others."* I'm going to say that it came from my Momma. She is the person I look up to because she is the epitome and example of putting self last.

What advice do you have for others?
My advice to others is that it's never too late to start chasing dreams. You are never too much or too little of anything. Don't put off starting to work toward your dream; don't do that to yourself. You never know whose life you're changing in the process.

Also, years after we are gone, my name and P.E.A.R.L.S. Mentoring for Girls, Inc. will be seen in the congressional book of records. We were recognized on the House Floor in Washington, D.C., on Thursday, November 20, 2020.

The Congressional Record is the official record of the proceedings and debates of the United States Congress. It is published daily when Congress is in session. The Congressional Record began publication in 1873 and is still published today.

Now, the entire world will be able to read about the excellent work we are doing in the Great State of Mississippi.

TROY BROWN, JR.
Age 30
Greenwood, MS
(Educator, Community Activist & Servant)

His affiliations include Providence Missionary Baptist Church, Omega Psi Phi Fraternity, Incorporated Beta Rho Chapter, Prince Hall Affiliated Mason, and the Elks IBPOEW Hart Lodge.

Beta Rho Chapter of Omega Psi Phi
On a typical spring day, April 18, 1962, the Omega Psi Phi Fraternity unveiled another light. In an impressive ceremony, before a general assembly of administrators, faculty, and students,

the Grand Basileus and Grand Keeper of Records and Seals presented a charter to eighteen (18) brothers authorizing the establishment of Beta Rho graduate chapter of the Omega Psi Phi Fraternity on the campus of Mississippi Vocational College in Itta Bena, Mississippi.

The Brothers of the Distinguished Beta Rho Chapter of the Omega Psi Phi Fraternity, Incorporated, were chartered in 1962 in Itta Bena, Mississippi. The Beta Rho Chapter and its over 62 members remain ever-committed to our Fraternity's international program of service, responsible citizenry, and community uplift. "Friendship is Essential to the Soul" is our Fraternity Motto, which serves to nurture the Omega Spirit. MANHOOD, SCHOLARSHIP, PERSEVERANCE, and UPLIFT are our Cardinal Principles, which together with our Fraternity Motto provide a framework for consecrated usefulness that has guided Beta Rho for over 58 years, and all Omega men since 1911.

What are you doing to bring awareness and spark change?
My goal has always been to be an advocate for children and my community. When I joined the Beta Rho chapter of Omega Psi Phi, Inc., it allowed me to continue to be an advocate but me in the company of great men that had the same goals and aspirations. Some of the things that we have done to spark awareness and positive change in 2020 alone include: building ramps for two elderly citizens, canvasing Leflore County with voter registration, awarding over $5,000 in scholarships, feeding teachers across Leflore, Humphrey, and Sunflower county for Teacher Appreciation Day, passing out masks and feeding essential workers, facilitating a Greenwood Graduate National Panhellenic Council, donating to Breast Care Awareness and Domestic Violence Awareness, volunteering at the Leflore Food Pantry, facilitating a city-wide Stop the Violence sit-down that consisted of over 60 men from our community, giving to victims who were impacted by natural disasters, participating in the 2nd Annual Black History Parade, being on the forefront of getting the confederate monument in front of the Leflore County House taken down, helping serve meals in surrounding counties and a plethora of other community-based projects.

Why have you committed to your cause(s)?
I believe as well as my chapter, that the youth in our communities should be afforded the same life experiences that we've had and more. What we do now sets the pace of what they can achieve in the future. Our commitment to friendship and helping our community is what binds all brothers of Omega together.

Who inspires you?
My parents and their activism have given me the blueprint on how I carry myself and my responsibility to serve those who look like me. They taught me that it's not the person's past that defines them, but their trajectory going forward.

What would you like to see happen as a result of what you are doing?

Our goal is to do our part in uplifting our community and the surrounding area through service and being actively involved in every aspect of good will. Our goal is to see Leflore County as the guiding beacon in what Black success looks like. We work because we believe that one day when we are gone, the future generations will benefit from the work that we do today.

What advice do you have for others?
Listen to the janitor the same way you listen to the President. A person's station in life does not dictate the importance of the information they can give you. You can learn from anyone.

What is your favorite quote?
"The tragedy of life is not found in failure but complacency. Not in you doing too much, but doing too little. Not in you living above your means, but below your capacity. It's not failure but aiming too low, that is life's greatest tragedy." Bro. Dr. Benjamin Elijah Mays

JERVIS MCGEE
Age 31
Itta Bena, MS
(Engineer, Hip Hop Artist, Producer & Manager)

Jervis McGee is a positive, young, ambitious man who thrives on helping others in hopes of creating better outcomes. He grew up in Itta Bena, MS, where he graduated from Leflore County High School in 2008.

Jervis received a football scholarship to play at Delta State University and graduated with a degree in Biological Science in 2012. He is a proud, responsible, and supportive father of Jervis McGee Jr. (14) and Haleigh McGee (6).
"I try to be a consistent role model each day." says Jervis.

Jervis works as a Quality Engineer for Smith & Nephew, and is responsible for maintaining the quality and effectiveness of orthopedics and pharmaceutical materials that assist people daily. He is also an independent Hip Hop artist who focuses on making feel-good music that people can relate to their lives. "I compose and write all my music to express how I feel through emotions and wordplay." said Jervis.

He has released five studio projects since 2017, ***Deference, Alter Ego, Just Because, Guilty by Association, Just Because 2,*** and is currently working on project number six, ***Progress & Profits***. His music is available on all the music platforms.

What are you doing to bring awareness and spark change?
I have consistently been leading by example with the moves and decisions I make to ensure my children and peers follow in my footsteps. I stand up for what is right by addressing issues in ways that will result in positive outcomes. Change does not happen overnight due to people not willing to change so easily. To get change, it will be more like running a marathon than a sprint. Consistency will play a vital part in whatever it is you want to change.

Speaking for myself, I try to express how I want to see change through my music and the actions I show in the community. Coming from a small town is motivation to help change the way people think and want to do better for their families. I have assisted with projects that gave back to my community and the surrounding areas in the Mississippi Delta.

Why have you committed to your cause?
My main reason why I am committed is to ensure my kids and the people after me will have a better future. I feel that one of the most important things that I can control is the involvement and influence that I can have on the outcomes of certain individuals. Hopefully, by staying committed, it would bring about the change that is needed to create a better future for the next generation.

Who inspires you?

My parents inspire me by how hard they worked to put me in the position that I am in today. Without those two, I would not be the man I am. They tried their best to raise me right while instilling great morals that helped me on my journey in life. I am incredibly grateful to have them as parents. They are the reason I am inspired to make them proud. I am the father I am because I pattern my parenting style after the way my father was with me. I am a loving person due to the way my mother loved me. They are my inspirations.

What would you like see happen as a result of what you are doing?

I would like to see a significant decline in violence and deaths in our Black communities. I would also like to see a drastic culture change and how today's issues are handled. People must realize what it will take to create a new space where we can live without fear and hate. The only way we can get there is by realizing that we have to want to change for ourselves.

What advice do you have for others?

Just remain true to yourself. Never let anyone or anything make you feel less of the person you know who you should be. Life is too short to worry about shortcomings and imperfections. No one is perfect, and also never take things for granted. The year 2020 was bad, and we all must be thankful for what we have.

What is your favorite quote?

"The greatest glory in living lies not in never falling, but in rising every time we fall. "-Nelson Mandela

DR. CHRISTINA A. R. GLADNEY
Age 32
Brandon, MS
(Founder of The Health P.L.U.G. (Prevention, Learning, Understanding, & Guidance, Founder of The Wellness Ministry, LLC, & Community Servant)

Dr. Christina A.R. Gladney is a native of Grenada, MS. Dr. Gladney is the daughter of Cassandra Perry and granddaughter of Mr. & Mrs. Bobbie Allen and James Gladney. Gladney graduated from Grenada High School in 2006 with high honors. Gladney received a Bachelor Science in Community Health Sciences in 2010 from The University of Southern Mississippi; a Master of Public Health in Epidemiology and Behavioral Science from Saint Louis University College of Public Health in 2011; and a Doctor of Philosophy in Health and Human Performance, with an emphasis in health behavior from the University of Florida in Gainesville, Florida.

After earning her Ph.D., Dr. Gladney returned to her home state of Mississippi with the mission of improving the health status of communities suffering from the lack of health education and health resources. In 2017, Gladney founded The Wellness Ministry, and currently serves as the Principal Consultant. The Wellness Ministry, LLC is a faith-based health consultant company serving North Mississippi churches and faith-based organizations through the coordination of health and wellness programs, services, and resources. In 2019, Dr. Gladney founded The Health P.L.U.G. (Prevention, Learning, Understanding, & Guidance). The Health P.L.U.G., a state-wide non-profit whose purpose is to promote health and wellness among Black men living in Mississippi and the greater southeastern region of the United States through culturally tailored programming and health education.
In 2020, Dr. Gladney served as the Interim Vice President of Enrollment Management and Student Services at Tougaloo College and currently serves as a Research Associate for the Office of Sponsored Programs and Research, providing leadership and assistance in grant writing and grant management college-wide. Dr. Gladney is a proud member of Alpha Kappa Alpha Sorority, Incorporated and currently active in the Beta Delta Omega Graduate Chapter located in Jackson, MS.

Dr. Gladney received leadership training as a member of the 2018-2019 cohort of the Mississippi Black Leadership Institute. Gladney was named the 2020 Philanthropist of the Year by the Black Alumni Gala of The University of Southern Mississippi. Gladney has also received national research awards for her doctoral dissertation on racial microaggressions among Black employees working at predominantly white organizations and her studies of the effects of father absence among adolescent girls and women.

How I have brought awareness & positive change:
- I feel that my God-given purpose in life is to educate and promote healthy behaviors among individuals and communities, especially those at elevated risk for cancer and chronic diseases. My first initiative after moving from Florida back to Mississippi was to educate faith-based communities about the eight dimensions of wellness (e.g., physical, emotional/mental, social, environmental, financial, occupational, intellectual, and spiritual), while offering resources and opportunities to establish or develop health and wellness ministries within their respective congregations. I provide assistance and support to churches in the area of health programming through the development of programs and activities to promote holistically healthy lifestyles.
- The second initiative was the creation of a non-profit organization, "The Health P.L.U.G.," which stands for Prevention, Learning, Understanding, and Guidance. The purpose of The Health P.L.U.G. is to create program initiatives and interventions that will improve the health and wellbeing of Black men living in Mississippi and the greater southeast. Understanding that many of the health issues present among Black men have cultural, economic, and social factors that influence the burden of disease in various aspects, it is important to address health among Black men from a holistic and Afrocentric approach. The first signature program for THP is Prostate *Positive*.
    - Prostate *Positive* was created to promote prostate health knowledge and behaviors that prevent prostate cancer among Black men in Mississippi. The purpose of Prostate *Positive* is to create a positive culture around prostate health. Often times, the prostate is only mentioned in the context of prostate cancer. The goal is to promote more conversations focused on primary prevention of

prostate cancer, rather than only detection, screening, and treatment.
- o The Health P.L.U.G. received funding through the Mississippi State Department of Health to deliver Prostate *Positive* presentations throughout the state. To date, there have been over 40 Prostate *Positive* presentations delivered to entities such as Mississippi Highway Patrol troops, job corps centers, National Pan-Hellenic Fraternities, local fire departments, local police departments, and male ministry groups in churches throughout the state.

Why have you committed to your cause?
- As stated above, I feel that health promotion and wellness education is my God-given purpose in life. I never imagined becoming a public health professional as a child. I knew I wanted to help people in the most significant way. Once I became aware of the field of Public Health and the area of health promotion, I fell in love with the concepts, strategies, frameworks, and theories. I knew this was the area for which God had called me because I have never had as much passion for another area of study. I continue to stay committed because of my Grandmother, who is my best friend. Unfortunately, she suffers from a host of chronic health conditions. She has had significant challenges over the years, including a stroke that left her paralyzed in her left arm and undergoing a triple bypass heart surgery. I strongly feel that if my grandmother had the health knowledge, resources, and support, many of the health conditions that are present would not. This is why I stay committed. If I can prevent someone or a community from having to endure and suffer from health issues by providing education and resources, I would like to do just that!

Who inspired you?
- I am inspired by my grandmother, Mrs. Bobbie Mae Allen. She is the strongest person I know. She is also one of the most intelligent individuals that I have had the pleasure to meet. She inspires me because no matter the circumstance, she continues to keep her faith and push forward.

What would you like to see happen as a result of what you are doing?
- I would like to see healthy and happier Black communities. I would like to see men, women, and children empowered to live their healthiest lives from a holistic perspective. Health is not always the most popular conversation in many households and communities of color. My hope is that health and wellness will become a priority to Black individuals and families, which will increase the overall quality of life and life expectancy among our community.

What advice do you have for others?
- Purpose is everything. Understanding who you are and whose you are is the first step in finding and living in your purpose. You can lose sight of your purpose focusing on the expectations of others and money, which is why it is so important to focus on purpose and allow God to open the doors for opportunities and elevation.
- If you wake up one day and want to do something totally different, do it. Dreams should be so big that you need God to make them come true!

Favorite Quote:
- Live with Purpose, On Purpose (Dr. Christina A.R. Gladney)

LATRICE SMITH
Age 38
Greenwood, MS
(Community Servant, Advisor for P.E.A.R.L.S. Mentoring for Girls)

Latrice Smith was born and raised in Greenwood, Mississippi. She is the daughter of Lucile Smith, sister of Tarren and Alton Smith, and mother of a son named Rashad.

While her brothers excelled in sports growing up, Latrice excelled in academics. A product of the Greenwood Public School District, she graduated number 11 in her class from Greenwood High School in 2001. After graduation, she attended the University of Southern Mississippi. During her time at Southern Miss, she participated in organizations such as the African American Student Organization, IDEAL Women, and Alpha Kappa Psi Business Fraternity. She also volunteered for Habitat for Humanity.

In 2005, Latrice graduated with a Bachelor of Science Degree in Business Administration. After her college graduation, she worked numerous jobs but didn't quite find what she was passionate about until she was introduced to P.E.A.R.L.S. Mentoring for Girls, Inc.

P.E.A.R.L.S. Mentoring for Girls was founded by Aisha Saffold in 2015. Aisha started the organization to mentor young teenaged girls in her hometown in Holmes County, Mississippi. As the need for the organization grew, Aisha decided to venture out to other counties. She met with ladies who were interested in mentoring, but it almost didn't happen. The woman that was going to be the advisor had to move away suddenly. Yet it was meant to be because another lady named Stella contacted Aisha. Aisha decided to give Leflore County a chance.

In 2016, the Leflore County Chapter began. P.E.A.R.L.S. Mentoring for Girls Inc. is a mentoring organization for young girls ranging from ages 10-18. We believe in our motto that every girl, no matter her zip code, deserves to fulfill her utmost potential. Our goals are to make sure our girls know their worth and let them know that they can achieve their hopes and dreams.

The organization conducts programs to instill the P.E.A.R.L.S. values: Purity, Empathy, Awareness, Respect, Leadership, and Scholarship. Since we began in 2016, the Leflore County Chapter has hosted an etiquette training session where the young girls learned how to set a table, napkin, plated placement, ordering, and appropriate table communication (table etiquette). We participated in the MLK March for P.E.A.R.L.S. Day On, which is a day of service devoted to the works of Dr. Martin Luther King Jr. We spent time with and painted the nails of the female residents of

Crystal Health and Rehabilitation Center. To instill sisterhood and unity, we treated our girls to spa treatments done by the mentors. We hosted the Mother-Daughter Tea in Itta Bena, Mississippi, where funds were raised for the organization.

During the latter part of 2016, Latrice was awarded the "Mentor of the Year" award. In 2017, she became the advisor of the Leflore County Chapter. Under her leadership, the chapter hosted the Pearling Ceremony, where our membership in girls doubled.
The Leflore County Chapter has produced the first and second Miss Pearls Extraordinaire. The chapter initiated and hosted its Women of Excellence program, where it recognized 12 successful Black women of the Mississippi Delta.

Who inspires you?
Inspired by strong Black women such as her mother and the former First Lady Michelle Obama, Latrice has always believed in encouraging sisterhood and going after what she wants to achieve. P.E.A.R.L.S. allows Latrice to commit to encouraging young girls to embrace a sisterhood while enabling them to be themselves without judgment.

What is your favorite quote?
"Whatever you do, be about it and do it with gusto."
It simply means whatever you're investing your time and energy into, embrace it and enjoy the experience.

Currently, the Leflore County Chapter is flourishing with 9ninementors and 24 mentees that are successful in academics and becoming more confident daily.

NIEMA JONES-STRONG
Age 40
Itta Bena, MS
(Owner of Bea Unique Salon, Cosmetologist,
Community Activist & Volunteer)

"Oftentimes, we only focus on our imperfections. We are less likely to concentrate on our unique abilities and what makes us powerful. The talents and traits that set us apart are usually what open doors of opportunity." -Niema Jones-Strong

Dark Emotions

At an early age, I knew I wanted to be a hairstylist. I had a dream of owning a salon, and I had a plan to get there. My plan was to get a degree in business, as well as obtain my cosmetology license. After high school, I began as a business major at Mississippi Valley State University. After my freshmen year, I decided to enroll at Delta Beauty College in Greenville, MS. The plan was to finish beauty school then go back and finish my degree in business. After earning my cosmetology license, I could style hair part-time while completing my degree. But first, I had to figure out how to get to Greenville every day for the next 15 months because I didn't have a car. I wasn't going to let the lack of a car keep me from finishing what I started. After catching rides up and down Highway 82, I successfully acquired my cosmetology license in Mississippi in 2000. Now, it was time to move to the next step in my plan.

I re-enrolled at MVSU, but I was also styling hair part-time out of my mother's house. However, due to the constant client traffic, doing business out of my mother's home was no longer an option. She forcefully told me, "find you somewhere to go." So, I was fortunate to be able to work in the salon of another local stylist. There I learned many more skills and much more about the salon business. I will be forever grateful for that time and experience. I also graduated with a bachelor of science in business administration from MVSU during this time. After four years, I felt it was time for a new chapter in my career.

In 2004, I opened my salon, Bea Unique. Bea is in homage to my maternal grandmother and family matriarch, Mamie Bea Jones. This move was definitely one based on faith. And I have certainly faced a fair number of tests of that faith. My first salon location had a substantial roof leak. If it rained the night before, we would get up extra early the next morning to mop up the water before the clients came in. If it started to rain while someone was there, we would put buckets out to catch the water. Yes, it was embarrassing, but at the time, I had to do what I had to do until I could do better.

I started my salon when I was a young woman, and I have grown tremendously over the years. I am excited about where my business is headed. I am more committed than ever to expanding the Bea Unique Beauty brand. I feel blessed and privileged to be a thriving Black female entrepreneur 20 years after completing cosmetology school. I am forever indebted to my family and community who have supported me throughout my journey. As I embark on the next phase of my career, I also want to help others realize their own potential.

Recently, I selected five young, ambitious girls in middle and high school who aspire to be entrepreneurs. As their mentor, I teach them that success is a slow and steady process that requires discipline and commitment. I want them to follow their dreams and make their own path. We also spend time discussing growing into womanhood, entrepreneurship and sharing their gifts with the world.

I am also proud to volunteer through my sorority, Delta Sigma Theta, Incorporated. I have also volunteered with the Fannie Lou Hamer Cancer Foundation, Leflore County High School, MVSU Learn to Swim Program, and Complex Solutions, LLC. I firmly believe to whom much is given, much is required. Therefore, I will always find ways to be of service to my community.

A family of hard-working women raised me. From childhood into adulthood, I saw my mother and aunts working hard and making the best out of the hands they were dealt in life. They always surrounded themselves with successful women and desired a better life for their children and families. These women taught me that whatever I desired was within my reach.

1 Corinthians 3:7 states, "It's not important who does the planting, or who does the watering. What's important is that God makes the seed grow." I share my story as a testament to being resilient in the pursuit of my dreams while having faith in God and trusting him to increase my vision.

DENISE PITCHFORD
Age 42
Greenwood, MS
(Educator, Community Servant)

Denise Pitchford was born on December 25, 1978, to Mary Pitchford Woodley and James O'Neal. She currently serves as a middle school science educator. She has also served as an adjunct instructor for Mississippi Valley State University (2012-2016). This summer, she served as a medicinal delivery driver for Downtown Drugstore of Greenwood, MS.

 As the proud mother of Cassidy and Caiden, Denise still manages to wear man hats. She is the acting secretary of Lampton Memorial A.M.E. Church in Tchula, MS, Vice President, Youth Sponsor and Activities Coordinator for Theta Pi Zeta Chapter of Zeta Phi Beta Sorority, Incorporated, President of the Greenwood-Leflore

Association of Educators; Elections Committee Secretary for the Mississippi Association of Educators; and a 17 plus year Science educator wearing numerous these hats just seem to fit her style.

Denise is a proud graduate of the class of 1997 of S. V. Marshall High School in Tchula, MS and 2001, 2005, and 2008 graduate of Mississippi Valley State University in Itta Bena, MS. She enjoys spending time dreaming of retirement but is often found working and bonding with the elderly and disabled, or resting.

Her motto is, *"I'll do it because somebody has to do it."*

"I am honored that someone nominated me. My goal is to focus on the female youth. In my sorority, I serve as a Youth Sponsor. In this role, I want young ladies to feel free to talk among themselves, engage in service (focusing mainly on the elderly – our forgotten heroes) and strive for academic growth. Under my service, we have placed first and second in ZHOPE (Zetas Helping Other People Excel – community service) for the past three years, even earning myself Regional Youth Advisor of the Year in 2018." said Denise.

For many years, she has devoted a lot of her time and attention to promoting Science Fair competitions. She has worked to seek outside sponsorships that expose the youth to the need for science and give opportunities for them to compete on levels that provided broad exposure in hopes of them "seeing" the world outside of their community.

Why have you committed to your cause(s)?
My reason for commitment is simple --- when I am elderly, WHO will take care of me? The things I instill in my youth and hopefully the students that I teach are the platform for my future doctors, lawyers, leaders in general. I hope to build a foundation that keeps on building. (I guess it is safe to say that I see a little fruition: several of my co-workers were my former students who were influenced into the teaching profession, and a few (who once professed to "hate science" now have careers in the science field.)

Who inspired you?

In the words of the elders, I "broke my leg" when I was 14 and recall my grandmother, Lille E. Pitchford, saying, "Do something first, then make a family. Not everybody gets a second chance." So, I guess my inspiration, the person who inspired me, was my Grandmother.

What would you like to see happen as a result of what you are doing?

I hope to see fewer teen pregnancies, more college graduates, and --- on a small level --- more confident, respectful youth. My wishes, dreams, goals, ... they're small. I just want a better community.

What advice do you have for others?

My advice to others is, "Invest in a child." Be it time or money; you would be amazed at the difference it makes.

Being a single mother of two, with one child having a heart condition while trying to balance the role of caregiver to my legally blind mother and stay on top of my organizations, is challenging.

Over the years, many of the students ask of my son because they remember my being out for his surgeries or getting called to his school because of an "emergency." Some have said that they are amazed when they see him because you wouldn't know by looking at him.
Now, he's walking (5 years) and talking (2 years) and eats a bit by mouth. We've come a long way!

TOPAZ THORTON
Age 46
Fort Worth, TX
(Educator & Radio Host)

Topaz Ingram Thornton, originally from the small East Texas town of Daingerfield, has been an educator with the Dallas and Fort Worth Independent School Districts for the past 24 years as a High school English and AVID teacher, Academic Coordinator, Assistant Principal, and Dean.

Topaz currently holds a BA in Psychology with a minor in Biology from the University of North Texas and M.Ed. in Educational Leadership from the University of Texas at Arlington with Principal Certification.

Topaz's passion for pouring into and cultivating the whole child & propelling them into their purpose, while undergirding families, has been her mission for over two decades. Topaz also serves as an Elder in her local church. She facilitates Brave Women's small group bible studies, and leads a ministry that educates parishioners about their Spiritual gifts, personality, passions, and abilities in spiritual environments & settings.

Topaz birthed Mirror On The Wall Ministries, which encourages and equips believers to live a victorious and successful life in Christ. She enjoys hosting two radio shows, "Spiritual Cocktails" on Facebook and "Mirrors and Microscopes" on the Impacting Leadership Network.

She has three children Taylor (Artist & Entrepreneur), Andryia (Hospital Corpsman in US Navy), and Artist III (Computer Animation Major).

What are you doing to bring awareness and spark change?
Some of the things that I do to bring awareness and spark positive change are joining and impacting small groups through teaching & discipleship, share nuggets and encouragement on social media platforms and radio networks, serving in my local ministry, speaking engagements & workshops, and mentoring young adults.

Why have you committed to your cause(s)?
There's nothing more frustrating, than living and navigating through life feeling lost and unsure. I know what it feels like have people around you, but not pouring into you. I know what it feels like to know you have potential but don't have much guidance or know exactly what to do with it. I know what it feels like to choose a life of self-destruction, self-sabotage, and irresponsibility because you have no purpose or direction & decide to just remain

in darkness & the wilderness. So, because I've walked that path, I desire to support and encourage others to explore their gifts, purpose, and dreams so they can choose a fulfilled life, not one that's a bi-product of confusion.

Who inspired you?
I don't have a role model per se. I've always admired the strength and fortitude of my grandmother and great-grandmother. They were always loving, open, accommodating, and carried a quiet strength. They weren't loud or boisterous, but were prayer warriors whose words carried weight, when they were compelled to speak. Their life reminded me of the ministry blueprint, model, and love of Jesus. Which is truly my model and ultimate inspiration...to love, live, & lead like Him.

What would you like to see happen as a result of what you are doing?
My goal and mission are that once others discover their purpose and gifting, that they feel compelled to help others to bring about awareness. The more we know about ourselves and what we bring to the table, the more authority we'll have to choose a path that aligns with God's purpose, not someone else's vision or idea of our purpose.

What advice do you have for others?
After you discover your God-given purpose and are confident in who you are authentically, do not deviate from that. Your success, victory, and celebrations should be derived from who you truly are, not who you pretend to be.

What are your favorite quotes?
"I've learned that people will forget what you said, people will forget what you did, but people will never forget how you made them feel." - Maya Angelou

Philippians 4:8, ESV: *"Finally, brothers, whatever is true, whatever is honorable, whatever is just, whatever is pure, whatever is lovely, whatever is commendable, if there is any excellence, if there is anything worthy of praise,* **think** *about* **these things.***"*

DERANDIUS SIMMONS, SR.
Age 47
Memphis, TN
(Owner of Simmons Transport, LLC. & Brother's Lawn Service)

I, Derandius Simmons Sr., am the husband of Sabrevian Simmons. We have eight beautiful children and eight amazing grandchildren. In 2007, we started Brother's Lawn Service, where we did detail professional landscaping. At that time, our teenage boys were growing more knowledgeable of the business. After being in the lawn business for five years, I decided to venture out and head in a different direction.

In 2011, I decided to attend school to obtain a commercial driver's license. Once received, I spent a lot of time driving on the road. After traveling and thinking about how to ensure more financial security for my family, God gave me a vision. In 2017 the journey to establishing Simmons Transport LLC began. I'm happy to say that taking a chance and accomplishing my goals allowed me to become a successful and productive business owner. My family and I are now expanding and growing, and we give all of the praise and honor to Jesus Christ.

Who are your most significant influences?

Everything that I have experienced and encountered during my life has pushed me to want to be better each day, from my upbringing to the smallest bits and pieces of my life. Everyone and everything have been a significant influence. I don't consider there to be any big "I's" or small "u's". I say this is because GOD has put before me good and bad experiences contributing to who I am today.

What are your future goals?

My future goal is to become a better me. I want to be a better father, husband, and man. I want to be the BEST me that God has equipped me to be! Placing GOD as the leader in my life will allow me to maintain these goals. I learned in time that any goal I wanted to achieve couldn't be achieved without God's guidance. My career goal is to expand our family business Simmons Transport LLC. ten times greater with the help of GOD. I want to be able to leave a legacy for my family and honor to my family name.

What do you attribute to your success?
Love, Loyalty, and GOD

What advice do you have for others?

The advice I would give to people: Give your life to the LORD. Listen and respect the older generation while you have them. Learn as much as you can. Never give up or allow a bad experience to make you believe you are lesser than the next person. Learn from your mistakes and utilize them to become a better you.

What is your favorite quote?
My favorite quote is *"Life in the pursuit of happiness."*

What are you doing to bring awareness and spark change?
One thing I have done to bring awareness is to share my experiences with other people. I offer my truths and let those I come in contact with know that there is a light at the end of a tunnel. Nothing is too hard for GOD. I share with them that I was a young man that experienced "three hots and a cot," and I beat the odds. I went back to school and started my businesses. I am proud of my accomplishments. First, it was Brother's Lawn Service est. 2007, and now my business has expanded to Simmons Transport LLC est. 2017.

Why have you committed to your cause(s)?
I am committed to making a difference in others' lives by being willing to give people an opportunity. I've learned that one opportunity can change a life. It helped change mines, and I will be forever grateful and willing to give back.

CLINTON GATEWOOD
Age 48
Greenwood, MS
(Mentor/Advisor, Educator, Coach)

Clinton Gatewood is married to Kimberley Jones-Gatewood, and together they have one son, Jorden. Clinton was born and raised in Greenwood, MS. He is a proud graduate of Amanda Elzy High School. He earned a Bachelor of Science Degree in Health, Physical Education and Recreation and a Master of Science in Environmental Science from Mississippi Valley State University. He also earned an Educational Specialist Degree in Educational Leadership from Arkansas State University. Clinton is currently working towards achieving his Doctorate Degree in Educational Leadership from Walden University.

Clinton is most notable in the sports arena. He currently oversees a school district's athletic department in his hometown, serving as the Chief of Athletics. He has also served as the Head Football coach of Greenwood High School since 2010. *"My biggest goals are to live a life that is pleasing to God, beneficial to my family and this community," says Clinton.*

What are you doing to bring awareness and spark change? One of the things that I have done to spark positive change is ensuring that I am active with the young men in the community. I have been coaching and working with young men in the athletic arena for more than 24 years. I have gained many sons from this position. The impact that I have made on these young men went beyond the football field. Many, I stayed in contact with, providing guidance spiritually, professionally, athletically, and academically. Throughout the state of Mississippi, I have helped over 150 kids enter college through athletics. In order to play sports, their academics must also be in good standing. I preach, *"A before B,"* *Academics before ball.* I have provided the guidance, discipline, and developed skills for each of these players to perform at the next level and become successful adults.

Greenwood has gradually become a town getting attention for high crime, primarily black on black crime. I want to be a guiding light for the young men in my community. I want to show them that they do not have to become victims or suspects in criminal activity to be known in this town. They can do something positive and be well known. It has always been a dream of mine to change young men's mindset headed down the wrong path.

I have a son. I know it's just as easy for my son to become a victim as it is for him to become a suspect. I am raising my son in a manner I would deem correctly. However, I also realize some young men do not have anyone to serve as a guiding light. I want to be that for them. Being that positive role model or mentor for them could also help save them from criminal activity, jail, and even death.

What would you like to see happen as a result of what you are doing?
I would like to see my community more united as a result of my impact. For years, we were divided by school districts. Now, that is not so. It is still very tense when we bring a group of young people from one side of town together with another. We are still having to take precautions with those things, and it should not be that way.

Greenwood's population is approximately 14,000. We should not be divided by a street name, a location, a school we attend, nor a color we wear. My hope is for all of us to be able to mingle together without the worry of violence or criminal activities taking place. **I want the violence in our community to stop~ allowing these young people to learn, make mistakes, and grow from them.** I want to see the adults do more to keep our kids actively involved in positive things.

What advice would you like to share with others?
My advice to others is that we all must be the change we want to see. Let us start being more supportive of one another so that we can be an example to our young people. Let us practice being honest with them and having conversations that they may not want to hear. We must break generational curses of our children finding their own way. Do not give up on them. If you cannot be the help the child may need, do not be afraid to reach out and tap into community resources or other individuals so they can better assist you and your family. The lives we save can very well be that of our own children.

What is your favorite quote?
"It's not how you start, but how you finish."
From the time you are born until the time you leave this world, there will be adversities and things that will hinder your progress. We will all make some mistakes, but how we use those mistakes in life is what matters. You can use them as lessons that will ultimately produce growth, or you can allow them to hinder you and keep you stagnated. The ending is always the most important!

LULA ELLIS
Fort Worth, TX
(Author, Activist, Poet, Talk Show Host)

Lula Carr, a Mississippi native, is a Poet, Actress, Minister, business owner, and Radio Host. Her resume includes a Bachelor of Arts degree in Sociology from Mississippi Valley State University. She also earned a Master of Arts degree in Professional Development from DBU in Dallas, TX, where she currently resides.

Lula currently serves as the host of an online radio show called "The Sistah Lula Show," which airs on Sunday nights. Lula's mission is to reach people all over the world who have difficulties coping with challenging situations. Through the power of prayer, which was instilled in her as a little girl, Lula believes she can make a difference in others' lives.

What are you doing to bring awareness and spark change?

In 2009 LEND ME YOUR EAR MINISTRIES was birthed to help needy families all over the world. My ministry started a prayer team, host events, and more. I've seen people learn how to adjust to change, come out of depression, make better choices, and become stronger through the word of God

Why have you committed to your cause(s)?
I've committed my ear, time, love, and resources to the cause.

Who inspired you?
The loss of my mother at age nine and never having a relationship with my father are my reasons and motivations for wanting to give ears to those struggling with loneliness.

What would you like to see happen as a result of what you are doing?
I'm hoping to see us go back to being a village. When one hurts, we all hurt. It's time we begin focusing on loving each other more, coming out of bondage, and working together.

What advice do you have for others?
Make the best of your moment and time in the season.

What is your favorite quote?
"My pain set me up for greatness." -Lula Ellis

PATRICIA A. YOUNG
Age 49
Itta Bena, MS
(Co-Pastor, Owner/CEO of School of Champions, & Community Activist)

Patricia Young has been married for 28 years to Mr. Curtis Young Sr. They have five beautiful children and eight grandchildren. She serves as the co-pastor at Lion of Judah Prophetic Ministry with her husband, Pastor Curtis Young Sr.

Patricia is also the Owner/CEO of School of Champions Development & Learning Academy LLC. in Itta Bena MS. She is the creator of the Founder of Youth Revolution Project, founded in

2014. It serves as an organization designed to mentor, tutor, inspire, and motivate young people.

She has worked as the Court Clerk of Itta Bena, MS, for eight years and has written grants for the city to help bring in revenue. She also advocates for Parents for Public Schools and is a member of the P-16 Council in the city of Itta Bena. "I'm also an advocate for change in utility system (light bills) in the City of Itta Bena." said Patricia.

"I have a real passion for women and children. Growing up in the City of Itta Bena, I've experienced many challenges as I grew up in the projects at 301 Sunflower Road Itta Bena, MS Apt10-B. God has been so good to me and has allowed me not to be a victim of my community but to be a game-changer." she said.
I'm inspired by many, but most inspired by Dr. Martin Luther King Jr.'s *"The Time is always right to do what is right."* And John Lewis, *"Never ever be afraid to make some noise and get in some good trouble, necessary trouble."* Positive change is what I would like to see happen in a small town where there looks like there is no hope. But I see Itta Bena as a diamond buried in the mud needing a fresh start. My advice to others is to be the change you want to see.

"You don't have to be great to start, but you have to start to be great."   *- Zig Ziglar*

"When obstacles arise, you change your direction to reach your goal, you do not change your decision to get there."- Zig Ziglar

"You were born to win, but to be a winner, you must plan to win, prepare to win, and expect to win." - Zig Ziglar

LINDA PAYNE
Age 51
Greenwood, MS
(Area Director for Special Olympics, Communication Director of Greenwood-Leflore Autism Spectrum Society, Community Volunteer)

Linda Payne is the Area Director for Special Olympics, which serves over 300 athletes. She is the co-founder of Grace2Serve Organization, which provides free turkeys to over 70 families during the holidays. She also serves as the Director of Communication for G.L.A.S.S., which provides support to families and individuals with Autism

Linda volunteers as part of the Delta Gems programs for the Greenwood-Itta Bena Alumnae Chapter of Delta Sigma Theta Sorority, Inc., which focuses on building character and providing support to young ladies in the local community. She also serves as a mentor to two young girls for P.E.A.R.L.S. of Leflore County organization for young ladies at risk in the local community.

Linda has diligently worked to ensure students with disabilities live an inclusive lifestyle during school, after graduation, in the community, and sports. She has also committed to supporting and educating family members and the community on the importance of including all students in the regular education setting.

"Our mother also has the heart to help young girls who need support and guidance reach their full potential in life."
– Linda's daughters

MIKE GUINN
Dallas, TX
(Professional Actor, Poet, Author, and Activist)

From Irving, Texas, Michael Guinn is an African-American Poet, Actor, Activist who has appeared on television, film, and stage.

His resume includes award-winning stage performances at the local, national, and international levels. He is a two-time national poetry slam finalist and international spoken word slam champion. Mike has transformed his life and his art in a way that has enabled him to coordinate several successful ongoing showcases, anthologies, high profile open mics, and workshops throughout the country. Currently, you can see Mike on the Amazon Prime Series: Peter Season One and Battle Lines. Mike is also the lead actor in the upcoming film God's Tired. Mr. Guinn holds a master's degree in social work and is on the frontlines full time daily as a youth mental housing coach in Dallas, Texas. Michael recently won the Irma P. Hall Black Theater Award for Featured Actor and is a judge for the NAACP Image Awards for Poetry. Michael has been twice nominated for Texas Poet Laureate. He is considered one of the state's most electrifying event emcees who often lends his expertise as a high energy host for special events and fundraisers. You can find out more about Mike's 22-year career by visiting HOME/ mikeguinn or googling Michael Guinn. Mike is not perfect, but his relentless drive to always be a professional whose on-stage experience and off-stage leadership makes him one of the country's most reliable speakers. Stay tuned. Mike has two global anthologies now in post-production.

FREDDIE WHITE-JOHNSON
Greenwood, MS
(Founder and President of the Fannie Lou Hamer Cancer Foundation, Co-Author, Activist)

Freddie White-Johnson is the daughter of the late Wilson V. and Earnestine White on a Plantation in Doddsville, Mississippi. Later, her family moved to Ruleville, MS. She has eight siblings, one of who is deceased.

Dark Emotions

She completed high school at Ruleville Central. She received her Bachelor of Science degree in Criminal Justice at Mississippi Valley State University, a Master's degree in Public Policy and Administration with a concentration in Urban Management and Community and Economic Development at Jackson State University, and done further studies at Jackson State University.

Upon completing graduate school, Freddie worked for the Department of Human Services, known as the Welfare Department as a case manager. She also worked for the Department of Social Work as a licensed social worker and a licensed Day Care coordinator. Upon leaving the Department of Social Service, Freddie took employment with Freedom for Hunger of Davis, California as a Community Facilitator in North Mississippi. After that, she worked for Delta Hills Public Health District – Mississippi State Department of Health as a District Community Health Coordinator.

Currently, Freddie is the Program Director for the Mississippi Network for Cancer Control and Prevention (MNCCP) at the University of Southern Mississippi. The purpose of the NETWORK is to build on an established community and institutional capacity to eliminate cancer health disparities by conducting community-based participatory education, training, and research. The goals of the NETWORK are to improve access to and utilization of proven beneficial cancer interventions.

She is the Founder and President of the Fannie Lou Hamer Cancer Foundation, a 501(c) 3 non-profit community-based organization serving 82 counties in Mississippi. The Foundation's mission is to reduce or eliminate disparities in the mortality rates of breast, cervical, colorectal, and prostate cancers in Mississippi. To that end, the Foundation concentrates on cancer awareness, education, research, advocacy, and increasing utilization of proven life-saving early detection screenings.

According to Freddie, growing up on a plantation in Ruleville, Mississippi, the daughter of a sharecropper, and losing my father to lung cancer gave her an insight into what I needed to do in life to become successful. She stated, her fight with cancer began in November 1977, when cancer took my father's life.

She stated, "My father, who had no education, was born, reared, and died in the rural Mississippi Delta where poverty is rampant, and healthcare coverage didn't exist. During that time, when the economy was slowed, and the cost for healthcare was escalating, underserved Delta residents (including my father) paid the price through reduced life expectancy and higher rates of cancer and heart disease.

On his death bed at the hospital in Clarksdale, MS, he said to me, "Freddie, you need to get a good education and use your education to make a difference by helping the poor people." Since my father's death, I have chosen to become an advocate for the underserved, as I once was.

Within a short distance of Mrs. Hamer's birthplace in Ruleville, Mississippi, Freddie spearheads national fundraising to help purchased two acres of land for the future headquarters of the Foundation that will also include a regional institute for the promotion of cancer awareness, education, physical activity, a healthy diet, and early detection. In 2012, Freddie solicited key stakeholders' support and launched a $2.5 million capital campaign for the Fannie Lou Hamer Cancer Foundation's state-of-the-art headquarters, a 10,000 square-foot building. In April 2014, the state of Mississippi awarded $300,000.00 to the Fannie Lou Hamer Cancer Foundation to help with the construction of the foundation. Freddie has built a solid partnership with local, state, and national agencies to address cancer disparities and their underlying causes. In October 2013, Freddie launched a national fundraising project called **"Cookies to Defeat Breast Cancer."** The proceeds from the cookies sales were used toward the construction of the Foundation's headquarters.

In July 2014, Freddie developed and launched the Fannie Lou Hamer Cancer Foundation's specialty license plate. She applied for a historic specialty license plate to help further raise awareness of the issues of cancer as well as to raise funds to support the construction of the foundation's headquarters, which will be located in Ruleville, MS – the hometown of the Late Civic Rights Leader, Fannie Lou Hamer who died from untreated breast cancer. The Mississippi legislature approved the specialized license plate in commemoration of the late civic rights leader, Fannie Lou Hamer, who died from untreated breast cancer.

The license plate was signed into law on April 22, 2015, by Governor Phil Bryant.

Freddie has written and received grant awards to address cancer health disparities. She has received more than $300,000.00 in grant awards from the Avon Foundation's Breast Health Outreach Program.
To help fight cancer health disparities, she has solicited and received financial and/or in-kind support from the City of Greenwood, City of Ruleville, County Board of Supervisors in Leflore, Sunflower, Holmes, Bolivar, Washington, and Humphreys county. She received $25,000 from the Tallahatchie County Correctional Facility and has raised more than $1.3K to address cancer health disparities in rural communities in the Mississippi Delta and for the construction of the Fannie Lou Hamer Cancer Foundation's headquarters.

Governor Phil Bryant selected Freddie to participate in the 2014-2015 Delta Leadership Institute.

Also, in Freddie's work over the last 15 years, she has established a profound network between welfare agencies, healthcare providers, local and state political leaders, businesses, universities, faith-based groups, civic organizations, and most of all with the community residents to fight cancer and health disparities. She stated, "These experiences have provided me with a unique set of skills that allows me to work at the individual, community, academic/researcher, and funder levels. I am committed to improving the health of Mississippians."

Freddie has trained more than 1,000 adults (men and women) Community Health Advisors (CHAs) known as volunteers and more than 50 high school girls as Junior Community Heath Advisors (J-CHAs). Through her work with the Fannie Lou Hamer Cancer Foundation, she has trained volunteers in 22 counties.

Freddie developed and implemented a pilot program, "Community Health Advisors (CHAs) Men in **Black** and **Blue** Fighting Prostate Cancer" in Greenwood, Leflore County, Mississippi. These trained men strive to help other men to take a proactive approach to their health and encourage them to discuss prostate cancer risk factors and testing options with their physician. They work to save lives, provide educational information to prostate cancer survivors, educate those at risk, and work with medical providers to conduct free or reduced prostate cancer testing rates.

- She has trained more than 100 African American men as Community Health Advisors – Men in Black and Blue Fighting Prostate Cancer;

- She has assisted more than 500 men who have rarely or never been screened for prostate cancer. And six of those men were diagnosed with prostate cancer.

- She has identified and assisted more than 2500 women who have rarely or never been screened for breast cancer, whereas 80 of those women were diagnosed with breast cancer.

- She has trained more than 1000 women as Community Health Worker as Research Partners (CHARPs) in 10 counties (8 in the Mississippi Delta and two counties in South Mississippi)

Positions and Honors
Other Experience and Professional Memberships
Former Board Member, Reach US- Mississippi
Salvation Army, Leflore County; Board Member
United Way of Leflore County; Former Board Member
Former Board Member, FEMA of Leflore County
Former member, Mid-Delta Home Health's Professional Advisory Committee (PAC); Advisory Member
Lifetime member, Alpha Kappa Alpha Sorority, Inc.
Mississippi Partnership for Comprehensive Cancer Control (MP3C); State's Board Member
Former member, Mississippi Partnership for Comprehensive Cancer Control; Chair, Delta Region
Former Board Member, Greenwood Leflore Hospital

A few of the many awards and honors presented to Freddie

2000	Received the State of Mississippi Senate Resolution for Community Health Leadership
2003	Community Service Award- Southern Eastern Regional of the Alpha Kappa Alpha Sorority, Inc., Jackson, MS
2004	Citizen of the Year- Beta Rho Chapter of Omega Psi Phi Fraternity, Greenwood, MS
2005	Drum Major for Justice Award- 21st National Holiday Honoring Dr. Martin Luther King, Jr., Greenwood, MS
2005	Citizen of the Year – Omega Psi Phi Fraternity, Inc., Mississippi State Organization Beta Rho Chapter, Jackson, MS
2005	Outstanding Community Service and Health Award – National Cancer Institute
2005	Outstanding Community Service in the Field of Health Award- Iota Delta Omega Chapter of Alpha Kappa Alpha Sorority, Inc., Clarksdale, Mississippi
2005	Governor's Initiative for Volunteer Excellence (GIVE) Award- Jackson, MS
2006	Greenwood's Voters League Award
2007	Prevention of Cancer in Mississippi Award- The Mississippi Partnership for Comprehensive Cancer Control, Jackson, MS
2008	Making a Difference in Rural Health Communities Award
2009	Received the Presidential Who's Who Among Business and Professional Achievers Award
2009-2010	Parent of the Year Award- Leflore County School District
2011	Received Community Health Service and Leadership Award presented by Tallahatchie County's Community Health Advisors
2011	Making a Difference in Healthcare Award presented by the Holmes County's CHAs
2012	REACH US Community Service Award presented by My Brother's Keeper, Inc.
2012	Received the Rural Health Champion Award presented by the University Mississippi Medical Center

2013	Received the Community Service Award presented by Alpha Phi Alpha Fraternity
2013	Received a Proclamation from Governor Phil Bryant for Establishing the Mississippi Law Enforcement Fighting Crime and Cancer Month
2014	Received the Humanitarian Award presented by Kappa Alpha Psi Fraternity
2015	Received the Mississippi Partnership for Comprehensive Cancer Control's Spirit of Giving Award
2017- 2020	Appointed to the Patient-Centered Outcomes Research Institute's (PCORI) Advisory Panel on Patient Engagement
2017	Appointed to the Greenwood-Leflore Hospital Board
2018	Received the World's Greatest Pre-Mother's Day Community Service Award
2018	Received the Minority Health Leader Award from the University of Mississippi Medical Center and Mississippi State University
2019	Received the Leadership Award for Participation Rendered to the Greenwood Leflore Hospital's Board of Commission presented by the Greenwood Voter's League
2019	Received the Humanitarian Award presented by New Saint Phillip M.B. Church
2020	Received the Higher Purposes Award presented by Higher Purposes, Inc.
2020	Received the Patient-Centered Outcomes Research Institute's Patient Engagement Award

Freddie is the co-authors of several publications
PUBLICATIONS
1. Parham G, Hardy C, **White-Johnson F.** Strategies for community participation in Cancer Prevention. *Ethnicity & Disease.* 2003: 13(3) *S3*-S7

2. Partridge EE, Fouad MN, Hinton AW, Hardy CM, Lisovicz N, **White-Johnson F**, Higginbotham JC. The Deep South Network for Cancer Control: eliminating cancer disparities through community-academic collaboration. *Family and Community Health.* 2005: 28(1) 6-19.

3. Hinton A, Downey J, Lisovicz N, Mayfield-Johnson S, **White-Johnson F**. The Community Health Advisor program and the Deep South Network for Cancer Control: health promotion programs for volunteer community health advisors. *Family and Community Health.* 2005: 28(1) 20-27.

4. Hardy CM, Wynn TA, Huckaby F, Lisovicz N, **White-Johnson F**. African American community health advisors trained as research partners: recruitment and training. *Family and Community Health.* 2005: 28(1) 28-40.

5. Susan Mayfield-Johnson, Ph.D.; Danielle Fastring, Ph.D.; Melody Fortune, Ph.D.; Freddie White-Johnson, MPPA, *"Addressing Breast Cancer Health Disparities in the Mississippi Delta Through an Innovative Partnership for Education, Detection, and Screening."* The manuscript has been accepted by the Journal of Community Health for publication in 2016.

She is married to her best friend, Larry Kite Johnson. Together, they have one son, Larry Johnson, II (age 26), and one God's son she raised, Shakir Miller (age 27).

Freddie's motto is "Become a HERO and leave a LEGACY for others to follow – REACH one, TEACH one, and SAVE one."

SYLVIA CLARK
Age 52
Winona, MS
(Owner of Kinnectz Therapies, Member of G.L.A.S.S., Community Activist & Servant)

Sylvia Clark is the owner and CEO of Kinnectz Therapies. Kinnectz Therapies is a pediatric therapy company that offers occupational therapy services. Kinnectz Therapies also provides workshops on sensory, autism, and handwriting training.
She is a graduate of Northwest Community College. She earned a Bachelor of Science from the University of Mississippi and a Master of Science from Belmont University.

Sylvia is a loving and devoted mother to her son, LaQuentin Potts, and daughter Alison Crockett. She is a proud member of Mt. Moriah M.B. Church in Winona, MS. She is a long-standing and active member of Delta Sigma Theta Sorority, Inc. She also serves as an Alumni Board Member of Northwest Community College. She is a
proud member of the Greenwood Leflore Autism Spectrum Society (G.L.A.S.S.).

What are you doing to bring awareness and spark change?
- Spearheaded many voters' registration drives
- Served as a workshop facilitator on a state and national level for autism awareness and training
- Served as a Go Red for women advocate and service coordinator.
- Created scholarship opportunities at Northwest Community College
- Served as a Toys for Tots facilitator to seek store donations to distribute to children
- Served as Delta Gems and Delta Academy Co-chair to help members of Delta Sigma Theta mentor girls on money skills, self-awareness, and other issues
- Served on the Beautification Community Committee for the city of Winona, where I volunteer and get others to pick up papering their neighborhood

Why are you committed to your cause?
Everything I do, I do to be a servant to others. I want to inspire everyone and show them that they can be a beacon of light in their communities. I am committed because I want to see a mental, physical, and spiritual change in others.

Who are your inspirations?
My main inspiration is my mom, Alice Louise Clark, and my dad, Bennett "Bill" Clark. My mom taught me the importance of prayer and education. My dad taught me perseverance and having good work ethics.

What would you like to see happen as a result of what you are doing?
As a result of what I do, I would like to see a healthier community filled with young adults striving to follow their dreams.

I would also love to see a community helping each other more.

What advice would you like to share with others?
My advice to others is Keep God first, always help others, and follow your dreams

What is your favorite quote?
For there is always light, if only we were brave enough to see it. If only we were brave enough to be it.   ----Amanda Gorman

PASTOR MARILYN JONES
Greenwood, MS
(Mother, Educator, Founder of MTS Ministry School)

The Mission: It is to build up and lift up the Mississippi Delta one person at a time through the word of God whether in spoken, written or living form. We do this by equipping, empowering, encouraging, directing, and developing aspiring and seasoned ministers.

Why are you committed to your cause?
I am committed to this cause because the harvest is plentiful and the laborers are few. I also feel that we have not trained enough people to go out and help with this mission. It is our duty as

leaders to equip others to help win souls and work in the kingdom of God.

Who are your inspirations?
I was inspired by Mrs. Lillie Butler who was the Sunday School teacher of Providence Missionary Baptist Church of Greenwood, MS in the 1980's. Miriam and William Dockery were also great inspirations for me as a powerful duet in teaching Bible Class at Providence during the same time. I had always wanted to be a teacher and they help guide me to follow my heart as God was prompting me to do. So, I became a student of Theology and obtained the training necessary to help teach others the word of God. Therefore in 2014, MTS was opened and the first class began here in Greenwood, MS.

What would you like to see happen as a result of what you are doing?
I would like to see more lives changed and impacted through the word of God being taught by those who have been equipped or trained in his word. For it is 2 Timothy 2:15 that tells us to study to shew thyself approved unto God, a workman that needeth not be ashamed, rightly dividing the word of truth.

What advice would you like to share with others?
My advice to others would be for you to make your calling and election sure, for if you do these things, ye will not fall as according to 2 Peter 1:10. You need to also make sure your heart is in the right place at all times. Jeremiah Wells was my student that encouraged and inspired me to stick to teaching even though he is no longer with us, his spirit lives on in my heart daily. So, as I performed this interview as a former student it gave me great joy to nominate MTS and help others to see the jewel that God has placed in its Founder Pastor/Teacher Marilyn Jones.

I would like for this entry to be placed in your new Heroes of Black History because God used this unique and beautiful teacher to help change my life for the better and I am eternally grateful!

Humbly submitted by Paula Dotson

Dark Emotions

Visions of the Future
By: Dr. Mary McBride-Brown

They pointed and laughed as you labored and ran,
To enlighten and bring awareness to your fellow man.
Though many days you hurt, yet still firm you stood,
Often fighting back tears, trying to do good.

Hold your heads up and smile, because you did your best.
You stood tall, never gave up, so you passed your test.
God sent me to confirm that he's very proud,
Of your ability to withstand and not join the crowd.

It's because of your work, our future looks so bright.
While you toiled during the day, we were asleep at night.
Now it's time for us to do our part,
Because you've carried our loads from your very start.

Dear Heavenly Father,

We come to you asking for divine grace, mercy, and favor over the lives of our **Flame Keepers.**

We ask that you protect our inspirations. They are the reasons many of our obstacles were removed.

Let no weapon formed against them or their legacies prosper. Let every tongue that rises against them be condemned. The plans of the enemy against them are destroyed.

Block every lying, underhanded, and deceptive spirit sent against them. Erase the defamation and attempted assassinations of their characters.

Let your holy angels watch over them day and night. Bless every good thing that their precious hands touch.

We decree and declare your divine favor, peace, wisdom, understanding, love, and prosperity over their lives.

In the name of Christ Jesus, we pray. Amen.

JOANN BUFORD
Age 61
Greenwood, MS
(Educator, Entrepreneur & Cosmetologist)

Joann Buford has been a Christian Cosmetologist for 30 plus years. Mrs. Buford is a loving mother, devoted grandmother, and a dedicated educator. She strives for excellence in every aspect of her life. She believes in having divine order in her life. She is a class act.

Joann is a role model and strives to set examples of love, faith, Christian fellowship, and high morals and standards for women both young and older. Her works of love can be shown through the acts of kindness she has and continues to pour into her community in a very positive way. She is a modern-day matriarch to her customers and peers.

Mrs. Buford currently works in education yet still manages to be a strong, consistent cosmetologist who cares for her client's whole inner being. God has truly favored her career as an entrepreneur, and she wastes no time giving God complete control of her life. She is definitely an Unsung Hero, so let us sing her praises.

MIRANDA HODGE
Age 63
Greenwood, MS
(Co-founder of Greenwood-Leflore Autism Spectrum Society,
Retired Educator, Community Activist)

Miranda Hodge is a native of Cataula, GA, and a 1975 graduate of Harris County High School in Hamilton, GA. She is married to Sheldon Hodge Sr. They are proud parents of three adult sons.

Mrs. Hodge is a 1979 alumna of the now Columbus State University in Columbus, GA., and a 1991 graduate of Mississippi Valley State University in Itta Bena, MS with a BS in Health & Physical Education.

Dark Emotions

In 2007 she earned her National Board Teacher Certification, which certifies her until 2027. Her teaching career began in 1991 as a physical education teacher at Dickerson Elementary in Greenwood, MS. She continued until 202,0 when she retired as a physical education teacher at Threadgill Elementary School with the Greenwood Leflore Consolidated School District.

"Teaching was my passion as a young girl. As an adult, I loved being an elementary school physical education teacher. I learned that mothering and teaching my son with autism would be my greatest challenge as a mother and a teacher." said Miranda.

Autism or autism spectrum disorder (ASD) is a developmental disability that can cause significant social, communication, and behavior challenges. People with ASD may communicate, interact, behave, and learn in ways that are different from most other people. The learning, thinking, and problem-solving abilities of people with ASD can range from gifted to severely challenged. According to the CDC, autism affects an estimated 1 in 54 children in the United States today.

With her youngest son's birth in 1995 came great challenges that propelled both she and her husband into the world of Autism. Their son was diagnosed at age 3 with mild developmental delay and at age 5 with Pervasive Developmental Disorder Not Otherwise Specified (PDD-NOS), an ASD known as Autism. He was non-verbal and had a seizure disorder, in addition to being challenged in the areas noted above. Although they were surrounded by medical and educational professionals who were knowledgeable and caring as they worked with her child, the Hodges needed more. They learned that many families in Mississippi and other parts of the United States shared some of the same challenges that we faced.

- The early intervention program offerings were not fine-tuned to meet the specific needs of parents and their children.

- Insurance companies would not cover a number of crucial services that doctors recommended and parents needed for their children.
- The regular education teachers needed additional training to address the (ASD) inclusion students' needs adequately.
- Parents needed more training on autism and a support system with people who had similar challenges. We needed a viable network of supporters in the Greenwood area.
- We needed more therapeutic options (occupational therapy, sensory integration, Applied Behavior Analysis...) to be made available in the Mississippi Delta.

The Hodge Movement

In order to **bring awareness and spark positive change in the Greenwood area,** I realized that God had given us an open door, an opportunity for our needs to be a catalyst for change. This change would benefit all parents and caregivers of individuals diagnosed with an ASD.

In 2008 my husband and I founded the Greenwood-Leflore Autism Spectrum Society (GLASS), a non-profit autism support group dedicated to creating success in the lives of individuals with autism and other disabilities. The organization's goals are to support, educate, empower, and advocate for the needs of individuals with autism and their families. Our membership consists of parents, caregivers, and supporters of individuals diagnosed with an ASD or other diagnosed disabilities. I currently serve as president of the organization.

We hold quarterly support group meetings & workshops, where professionals in the area of ASD provide cutting-edge information, knowledge, and strategies covering a wide range of topics that families can implement at home and in the community.

Members also provide individual support and encouragement to parents who just need to discuss the challenges and concerns faced as parents of a child with an ASD. Parents are empowered through this process, which helps them to become knowledgeable advocates for their children and their families. Individuals with ASD also learn how to become more effective advocates for themselves. As advocates for positive change, we actively network with our representatives in the state legislature to promote legislation designed to benefit individuals with ASD and their families. We also network with local school districts, health-related agencies, and adult rehabilitation agencies to promote positive change in the community.

April is Autism Awareness month. During that time, we celebrate by hosting our annual Autism Awareness Celebration. It provides an opportunity for the community to come together in an atmosphere of fun, fellowship, fitness promotion, and service to broaden our knowledge of ASD and raise funds for G.L.A.S.S. This event is the only fundraiser. At that time, we also share what we have done in the community during the year and how those activities have impacted families of individuals diagnosed with an ASD.

Celebrating the success of graduating high school seniors with a diagnosed disability is at the forefront of our activities. Our organization provides book scholarships for those attending college, as well as other scholarships for individuals furthering their education through adult education programs, job training, etc.

I have committed to the cause of autism awareness because it was not until I birthed a child with an ASD that I began to understand the great challenges the children and the families face. I am a woman of faith who believes that nothing is impossible with God. With that as my motivation, I had to become more strategic and learn how to teach my child at home and work alongside his teachers and therapists. At the early stages of my son's life, I knew that I had to work overtime to help him to reach the developmental benchmarks that he lacked due to the autism.

Dark Emotions

Along the way, many people have inspired me. Among those is Temple Grandin, who was born in 1946. She was diagnosed as brain damaged as a child, was non-verbal until age 3 ½, and recommended for institutionalism as a child. Due to her mother's tenacity and a lot of hard work, she continues to promote positive change for those with autism at the age of 73. Grandin is a professor of Animal Science at Colorado State University, has a successful career, and is a prominent author and speaker on both autism and animals.

Kassie Carter inspired me as I observed her interactions with her son, who has autism. I did not know her when she would be at church functions and community events, and her son was right with her, enjoying his environment. It wasn't long before we got to know each other. Seeing her son walk across the stage to graduate from high school helped me see that milestone for my son. Kassie is a tireless advocate for the cause of autism awareness and our organization.

In 1998 when my son started speech therapy at Greenwood Rehabilitation Center, I met the lady that **I call my miracle worker**, Mrs. Connie Weyland. At the age of 3, my child slowly developed verbal communication skills. This decreased his frustration and reduced my stress. It was amazing. Mrs. Weyland taught me the strategies we needed to continue the work in our home and community. At that time, we did not have a computer. She encouraged us to purchase one and suggested some software programs. At that time, we used programs like; Reader Rabbit, Jump Start, Hooked on Phonics, and others. These programs provided visual cueing and focused on phonemic awareness. My son developed a great love for books and reading. All that he had to do was ask for a book, and I would purchase it. Picture reading developed into reading words. And my reward was hearing him speak.

I was inspired by Sylvia Clark, who also has a son with an ASD. My son was about five years old when Sylvia, his occupational therapist at the Greenwood Rehabilitation Center, worked with him. She was strategic and intense during their sessions. My young son accomplished many developmental milestones as she worked with him. I could call her and ask questions when challenges developed between our therapy sessions. One piece of advice really stuck with me. She said, "If he didn't have autism would you let him do that." I responded, "No," She said, then don't let him do it." She implemented and applied many of her strategies to real-world situations that we faced.

As a result of the work that my family and the members of GLASS are doing, I would like to see more parents reach out for help and support earlier in the process of determining that their child has a developmental disability. The emotional, mental health, and financial health of the family can be stretched to the limit, and more so, if the challenge of autism is viewed with shame and regret. For me, my support came from my family, my church, and our support group, and others. The resilience of families is at stake. Research from the National Institute of Health reveals that parents of children with an ASD have a higher divorce rate than parents who do not have a child with an ASD. As parents and a community, we should be more vigilant about celebrating the accomplishments and strengths of our individuals with disabilities, while at the same time acknowledging and working to help those individuals improve in their specific areas of weakness and challenge. We must help them find their place in the world, which can sometimes be a very cruel place when you are different from what is considered the "norm."

My advice for those with young children is to start at the earliest age possible with your child receiving Early Intervention services. Don't let the stigma of your child possibly having autism stop you from moving forward. You can't afford to wait to see if the child will just "grow out of it," as some might say. Start by discussing your concerns with your pediatrician. If that person is like our former pediatrician, Dr. Claudine Stevens, at the Greenwood Children's Clinic, you will be guided in the right direction. If, for some reason, you are starting the work when your child is older or even an adult, don't give up. Start with a medical professional and move forward. Your child's progress will amaze you and put the individual on the path to a happy and successful life.

One of my favorite quotes is that "nobody takes better care of you than you." One writer said it this way, "Remember that if you want to take the best possible care of your child, you must first take the best possible care of yourself." One of my favorite scriptures is John 9:3b NLT "This happened so that the power of God could be seen in him." And that's it for me, be a parent and do the work. God gets the glory.

Hope & Encouragement come when we least expect them.
A Good Samaritan & Three Guardian Angels
On one typical weekday morning in 2016, I was preparing to go to work, and my youngest son was preparing to go to school at Mississippi Delta Community College-Greenwood Center. My husband and oldest son had already gone to work. Each morning my youngest son would wait in the house until about 12:00noon until his transporter, one of the deacons from our church, would come to take him to school. I picked up my phone and left the house at about 7:05 am for work. At about 8:10, I was called to the office at school. The secretary said that I received a call and handed me the phone.

A lady who knew me and where I worked, called the school to say that she saw my son walking down Hwy 82 and was approaching the area near Scott Petroleum. My heart sunk. I remember that she said he was near the gas station. I asked her to get him to stay right there and that I was on my way. As I drove, my thoughts went wild to images of Rodney King being beaten by police and someone trying to pick him up or harm him. I didn't speak those thoughts out loud. I just prayed that he would be safe. When I arrived at the gas station, my son was standing in front of 3 Greenwood policemen. The situation was calm. The policemen were quiet and looked like guardian angels surrounding him. My son walked up to me with a phone in his hand and said in a calm tone, "You took my phone." I said, "OK." Then I hugged my son, as well as the policeman that was closest to me, and thanked them. The policeman that I hugged said, "We didn't do anything. You should thank that lady". Pointing to the lady sitting in her car, who was still watching him for me. I went up to her, reached inside her car, thanked and hugged her. It all happened so fast I didn't ask her name. She was my son's good Samaritan. We drove home, and we sat down. All I could do was just look at him, hug him, and thank God for putting good people in his path who protected him; one good Samaritan andthree3 guardian angels.

My son said that he was sorry. I told him that it was my fault, then we talked about what he should do if something like that happens again. I called his dad. He came home. I coded the phones so that they looked different. I told him that he can always use the house phone if he needs to, and I will come home for him. His response to my mistake was an example of the impulsiveness characteristic of some people with autism. We went back to work, and he waited at the house until 12:00noon until his transporter came to take him to school. After work, I picked him up from school.

He now wears a medic alert bracelet everywhere he goes.

BARBARA "TINA" GRAY
Age 66
Greenwood, MS
(Registered Nurse, Founder of "Me Too" Conference)

Barbara Gray is a loving daughter of Willis and Josephine Gray. She is a devoted mother to Queeta Gray and Willard Tate, Jr.

She began her educational journey in the Greenwood Public School system and graduated high school in 1973. She received a Bachelor of Science Degree in Biology at Mississippi Valley State University in 1977. In 1984, she received a Bachelor of Science in Medical Technology from Presbyterian St. Luke. In 1996, she received her Associate's degree in Nursing from Mississippi Delta Community College as a Registered Nurse.

What are you doing to bring awareness and spark change?

Positive change for me begins with positive sparks by being an active member of Providence Missionary Baptist Church, being an active member of the Greenwood Voter's League, and Founding/Sponsoring the "Me, Too" Conference. This conference targets girls ages 8 – 14. Its purpose is to give these girls factual information about the transition from a girl to a young lady. The information shared incorporates the physical, emotional, and mental changes during a female's transition. This conference has brought so many people from our community together, from all sectors. It has brought together professional, civic, social, educational, and women who have medical (both mental and physical, and spiritual expertise.

Why have you committed to your cause(s)?
I am committed to this cause because of the lack of resources in our community that are either limited or unavailable to these girls, which would help with their transition into womanhood. I believe that through this factual knowledge base, these young ladies will be more equipped to make more positive and sound decisions about their lives. And above all, it will increase their confidence and Love for Self.

Who inspired you?
I am inspired by "Me." Visualizing the mistakes I made because I lacked the resources I'm now working to provide for these young ladies. Remembering how hard it was to understand how I am supposed to walk "perfectly" without guidance from someone willing to explain the obstacles they encountered, that would help me with my transition from a girl to a young lady.

What would you like to see happen as a result of what you are doing?
I have seen the maturation of many young ladies who have come through, "Me Too." I am a witness to their positive life accomplishments. I hope and feel that "Me Too" was a positive influence on their journey.

What advice do you have for others?

My advice to others is to remember and share your journey. Give back so that your journey's negative path can be avoided in the path of another one's journey.

What is your favorite quote?
The Serenity Prayer
"God, grant me the serenity to accept the things I cannot change, courage to change the things I can, and wisdom to know the difference.

DR. MARY NASH ROBINSON
Age 68
Greenwood, LA
(Retired Educator, Community Activist, Motivational Speaker)

Mary Nash Robinson is a product of Caddo Public Schools, having graduated from Bethune Jr/Sr High School. She is the Salutatorian of the Class of 1970. She earned an undergraduate degree in Social Science and Speech Education at Grambling College. She began her teaching career in 1973.

She is married to Jesse Robinson, Jr., whom she met in first grade. They are parents of three adult children. They have two grandchildren.

Dr. Nash Robinson earned a master's degree in Educational Supervision and Administration from Louisiana State University in Baton Rouge, LA. She earned +30+ at LA Tech, Northwestern, and Centenary. She earned a doctoral degree in Christian Counseling and Psychology at Louisiana Baptist University, where her dissertation assessed whether a sampling of school principals was successful because they demonstrated FRUITS of the SPIRIT, consciously or unconsciously.

Dr. Nash Robinson was employed by the Caddo Parish School Board for 43 years serving in many capacities. She announced her retirement at the end of the 2015-16 school year.

Dr. Nash Robinson is a lifelong member of the Zion Baptist Church. She sings in the choir, is a member of the hospitality committee, a media team member, and assists the youth ministries.

She is the recipient of numerous awards, i.e., being names among "Women of Excellence" by the Shreveport Chapter of Sigma Gamma Rho Sorority, Inc., "Rare Jewel" by the membership of the Pleasant Hill Baptist Church, and the Meritorious Award by the Inter-Faith Theological Seminary for services rendered to those in need. She was recognized by the Morning Star Baptist Church and Airport Community Center during African History Month for contributions to youth/field of education.

She is frequently called upon as a motivational speaker to young people. She is an active host of social and civic organizations to include the Board of Directors, Social Justice Civic League, The Links, Alpha Kappa Alpha Sorority, Inc., and National Sorority of Phi Delta Kappa. She is actively involved with a litany of professional organizations. She works untiringly to ensure that her affiliations in/with these organizations offer scholarships to deserving high school graduates.

She is a certified Court Appointed Special Advocate (CASA) representing children in foster care in legal proceedings, worked as an independent HR consultant and as a parenting educator for the YWCA/Northwest LS. She was employed as an assistant to the Shreveport Mayor Ollie S. Tyler for a year prior to accepting the position of principal at Magnolia School of Excellence-Upper Campus in June 2018. The school's mantra is ORDER, TEACHING, LEARNING…EVERYDAY! The school performance score has since improved from failing to grade D, with a growth index of grade B. Her work, she believes, is and has always been ordered by God.

Dr. Nash Robinson believes in her heart that God blesses her so that she can bless others.

Why have you committed to your cause(s)?

I asked God early on and constantly to equip me for service, use me, and order my steps. I have not always wanted to go where HE sent me. I have experienced bouts of weariness; just wanted to go home, sit it out because I was convinced it was a gross waste of time. Who, in their right mind, wants to mediate, be judged behind a calling supposed to ensure equity of resources, opportunities, or advocate for justice? Every time I chose that path of less resistance, **something or somebody** happened to redirect, encourage and re-energize me.

Who inspired you?

My parents were not educated folks. My father was a freight truck driver before rigs had 18 wheels. My mother was a housekeeper for several prominent, professional families in communities across town. They were, however, adamant with regards to certain things; God as the source of strength, HE had plans for our lives, we were going to college, we would have careers, and would make lives for ourselves like those on television in more affluent neighborhoods. I had dedicated spiritual leaders, astute teachers who taught content, but cared enough to address preparation and skillsets for **real** life. I am extremely grateful for the personal, spiritual, and professional mentors in every era of my life.

What would you like to see happen as a result of what you are doing?

I hope that people will realize and interact in a matter explicit of the genuine belief that we are more alike than different and that everybody has something worthy, purposeful to contribute.

What advice do you have for others?

No fear! The best experience is "on the job, in the middle of a mess training." My mother would always say, "Don't be scared. You were called into it for a reason. Count it all joy and just do your best." I sorely miss my mother!

What is your favorite quote?

Dark Emotions

There are many; some inspirational, biblical, professional, motivational. But as I am observing the birthday of Dr. Martin L. King, Jr., I found that he once said, *"Use me, God. Show me how to take who I am, who I want to be, and what I can do, and use it for a purpose greater than myself."*

REV. JESSIE PAYNE, JR.
Age 74
Itta Bena, MS
(Preacher & Teacher of the Gospel of Jesus Christ)
"Preaching 41 Years, Pastoring 38 Years

"A Humble, Anointed, and Equipped Vessel of God."

Why is he an unsung hero?

Rev. Jessie Payne Jr is a man of true humility. He had a unique call into the ministry, one in which, he tried to run from and avoid. God slow-walked him down 41 years ago. He has been a changed man since that day in January of 1980.

Pastor Payne teaches and preaches with modern-day parables that reach all age groups. He lives the life that God has lovingly chosen for him to live. He prides himself in developing the youth through Christ and education.

Rev. Payne is one that stays and preaches from the Bible consistently as God has prospered him to do. There are many false prophets. They give you the feel-good sermons or sermons that pique the interest of the worldly human side of life.

On the contrary, God uses our pastor/father to stay focused on the Holy Bible. Yes, this man is our father. He has been toiling in his gift even before TV evangelism became popular, even before the store-front churches became Megachurches, before the internet and Facebook surfaced.

We know he is an unsung hero because God did not bring this author into existence until now to help publish such great works for the mere working-class people of the Mississippi Delta, thanks to Dr. Mary McBride Brown, who will leave a treasured legacy behind for many years to come!!!

THELMA COLLINS
Age 75
Itta Bena, MS
(Retired Educator, Former Mayor, Published Author)

Thelma Collins, the former Servant Mayor of Itta Bena, MS, entered her final retirement as of June 30, 2017. She was born in this small Delta community and was called by a higher power to help improve the living conditions in her hometown. She has been a servant of the community from August 1996 – July of 2000. After four years out of office, she decided that her vision had not been completed; therefore, she reentered the race in 2005 and served until 2009. Her servanthood came to closure on Tuesday, June 2, 2009. Yet, she was called again **beyond her understanding** to serve again in her community on July 1, 2013, and served without receiving a salary until June 30, 2017. Her calling into the mayoral office in July 2013 was contingent upon her willingness to be totally directed by her heavenly Father, who directed her not to receive a salary because the city was in such financial dilemma.

Her vision for the City of Itta Bena is to become a college town that is vibrant, healthy, and a place for growing up and growing old. As she faced many challenges in this small Delta community, she believed in the power of God. With hard work and a commitment to be a servant for the citizens of this poverty-stricken community, the potential of this community will ultimately flourish.

One miracle, among many that took place during her administration, was the fact that she inherited the city's IRS debt of more than TWO HUNDRED THOUSAND DOLLARS. The IRS placed a lien on the total city, and there was no way for this obligation to be met by this municipality because of the depletion of funds. After making many contacts with senators, representatives, IRS personnel, and the consistent prayers, God literally stepped in, and the IRS abated the entire indebtedness.

After completing her B.S. Degree at Mississippi Valley State University, she continued her education by receiving a Masters' Degree at Mississippi State University. She taught school for thirty-six years, was an adjunct professor at Mississippi Valley State University, and has served on many civic and spiritual boards and organizations. She has received numerous awards and certificates for community service. Although the recognitions have been numerous, she does not focus on recognition from man; however, her life will not be in vain as long as she passes on to others the blessings she has received. Her goal is to be a blessing to others as God has blessed her.

Mrs. Collins has been married to Rev. Johnny Collins for fifty-two years. They have one son, John Paul Collins, and five grandchildren. At this juncture during her retirement, her ultimate aspiration is to continue working to improve the livelihood of the citizens of Itta Bena and to develop a closer relationship with the Lord. She daily seeks God's guidance and listens for His next assignment for her life.

What have you shared to bring awareness and spark positive change?
- Served as the servant Mayor of Itta Bena
- Worked to improve the aesthetic appearance of the community
- Networked with other communities to bring new ideas to the community
- Traveled to other communities to ascertain needed equipment, police cars, and other needed items for the improvement of citizen services
- Wrote grants for city buildings, parks, and infrastructure
- Developed a Website for Itta Bena
- Worked with Mississippi Valley State University to bridge the gap between the university and the community
- Worked with community organizations
- Assisted with October Festival Activities
- Organized annual Christmas Parade
- Worked with the Chamber of Commerce to promote annual clean-up day in the community
- Organized the Itta Bena Community Coalition
- Organized the Ministerial Alliance
- Worked four years without accepting the Mayor's salary
- Worked with the IRS to abate a $250,000 indebtedness that I inherited from past administrations
- Worked to organize summer activities for the community youth
- Developed a smoke-free community
- Wrote a book entitled, <u>I CHOOSE YOU</u>

Why are you committed to your cause?
I have been committed to the cause of improving my community because this is my home, and I have always desired to live in a community that was pleasant and enticing for others to want to live in the community.

Who are your inspirations?
I have been inspired by my family and educational personnel.

What would you like to see happen as a result of what you are doing?
I would like for the young people in my community to be inspired to participate in leadership opportunities.

What advice would you like to share with others?
My advice for others is to dream of whatever God has placed in your heart. For all that I am and all I hope to become, I owe it all to my loving Father in Heaven. Therefore, my advice to others is to always lean and depend on God, for He knows the plans that He has for us. Pray without ceasing, and I can assure you that He will never leave you nor forsake you. If you wish to be successful lean and depend on a loving Father who is in Heaven.

What is your favorite quote?
"I can do all things through Christ who strengthens me."
 Philippians 4:13

Mrs. Collins's book, *"I Choose You: When the Change You Want is Found Within,"* can be purchased on amazon.com.

REST IN PEACE
from
Leflore County High School's
Class of 1996
Itta Bena, MS

DEVON YORK
July 23, 1978 – January 10, 2021
Age: 43
Douglasville, GA
(Mother, Entrepreneur, & Educator)

Devon was the CEO of York Empowers, LLC, an empowerment and consulting company specializing in holistic strategies that help others develop their inner gifts and talents to live the life they were destined to have. Devon worked in the educational arena for more than twenty years in various leadership capacities as a transformational leader. It was in those positions that developed her passion for empowering others beyond education. She continued to serve society as an Empowerment Coach, Educational Consultant, Millennial Mentor, and Transformational Speaker.

Devon's lifelong dedication to supporting young people stemmed from her work in the educational arena for more than 20 years.

During her career, she served in various leadership capacities such as Instructional Coach, Writing Coordinator, Response to Intervention Coordinator, Charter school administrator, and educational consultant.

Her experience and spot-on intuition were utilized to support individuals in embracing their authentic selves through professional, personal, and spiritual direction. In addition to founding York Empowers, Devon spent the past 15 years establishing chapters Girl Power, a youth group for young ladies between the ages of 11-18. In 2018, she founded the Destiny Institute. Through the institute, the girls were provided summer learning sessions and are taught skills in Self-Awareness, Leadership, Entrepreneurship, and College and Career readiness.

In 2021, Ms. York was planning to host Atlanta's first and largest "Let it Go and Get Free Expo" in June, where she would have been launching her Survival Guide for Teens and book Beyond the Bio.

Above all of her accomplishments, she was most proud to be a woman of valor after God's heart and a mother of three wonderful children, Giancarlo, Kennedy, and Destiny.

Creating Legacy
By: Dr. Mary McBride-Brown

When all of the glitz and glamour have gone,
And you're hoisted down from your thrown.
What will they remember about what you said,
As you held the microphone up to your head?

What will they say about the life you lived?
What did you contribute? What did you give?
Will your name forever ring on high,
As you take your wings and prepare to fly?

Or will your name simply be yesterday's news,
Because of the choices you decided to choose?
It's never too late to change what they see.
Let's begin today creating positive legacy.

Black Girl Transformation
By: Dr. Mary McBride-Brown

Hey little Black girl! How have you been?
The Lord told me you needed a friend.
So, I showed up to encourage you.
I know how you feel. I've been there too.
Hush little Black girl. Don't you cry.
It's going to get better. Let me tell you why.
I was shedding tears when I was your age.
I hated my image. My soul was enraged.
When an angel stepped in to sit with me.
God showed her just where I would be.
She listened and gave me words of advice.
No female had ever treated me nice.
So, I'm happy to have been sent your way.
I'm here for you. God told me to stay.
Right by your side until you can see,
The amazing Black woman God created you to be.

My Ph.D.
By: Dr. Mary McBride-Brown

My Ph.D. got a standing ovation,
Yet, only qualifies me to complete applications.
His Ph.D. doesn't require shirts with collars,
But still gets him more respect and dollars.

My Ph.D. doesn't equal her tears.
She doesn't even have to have all of my years,
To be considered for positions over me.
Yet still I need a Ph.D.

My Ph.D. brings sarcastic tones,
And working my brown fingers to the bones.
Yet you cut her some slack when she complains
Of heavy workloads and threatened migraines.

My Ph.D. comes with stipulations,
And intentionally tarnishing my reputation.
Still, you're happier with him sitting over me,
He brings nothing to the table purposely.

Your responses are gentle with her and him.
You bend over backwards to not offend them.
But you eagerly wait to crucify me,
Do I need to destroy my Ph.D.?

Teach Me to Fish

By: Dr. Mary McBride-Brown

Oh, how I wish that you were here to fish with me again.
I thought the times we were together would never ever end.
You made me feel as if I were the best fisherman in the world.
Our times together were like opening up oysters filled with pearls.

You carried me on your back as you strolled down the banks.
You always prepared a seat for me by gathering smooth planks.
I never had to worry because you'd always bait my hook.
You were always there to watch my pole and tell me when it shook.

You even reeled in my catch and placed it in your cooler.
Your hands were always rough, but you made sure mine were smoother.
As the sun set, you carried me back up the muddy banks,
With dirty fish and poles in hand and even those smooth planks.

Like clockwork, I was knocked out as soon as you got behind the wheel.
Straight home, you rushed to clean the fish and prepare for me a meal.
My belly full as I rushed to bed to sleep the whole night through.
Just to wake up the next day and go back fishing with you.

Surprisingly you stayed asleep. Never thought our good thing would end.
Now I'm alone, and there's no one to catch fish for me again.
All those years, I should have learned how to prepare my own dish

Dark Emotions

As you read my poem, "Teach Me to Fish," I hope you found its intended lesson. Too often, we make the mistake of caring for people so much that we neglect their needs during the process. I have worked as a young adult supporting myself through college and as an educator in the Mississippi Delta for about 24 years. I have always done my best to teach the people God placed before me how to fish. I can feed the people and make them happy, but if I genuinely want to see them progress, I have to share my fishing knowledge with them. I need to make sure they know the intricate details of fishing. They also need to understand how to clean and prepare the fish for eating. To be able to catch fish and still not know how to clean and cook them is pointless. All the people will have are a bunch of stinky fish. Not only do they need to know how to cook them, but also how to preserve the leftovers for further consumption.

Dark Emotions

Quietly Unbothered
By: Dr. Mary McBride-Brown

Why are we so quietly unbothered by the injustices we see?
Black on Black crime may not matter to you, but it bothers me.

Our sons are killing each other, and no one seems to care.
Our daughters are growing up too fast. They need two responsible parents there.

The media keeps reminding us we're viewed as a disgrace.
As we sit quietly unbothered, watching the destruction of our race.

We're crucifying academics while glorifying athletes.
Not taking the time to understand our children need to compete

Intellectually with the world, so they'll have a running start
To make it to the finish line and show the world they're smart.

But it doesn't bother us one bit that the world can see
Just how quietly unbothered we are to accept mediocrity.

It hurts to support Black businesses or promote creative Black art,
But we'll gladly stand in long lines buying equipment from Walmart.

We easily get loans for cars but never qualify for a home.

Dark Emotions

This doesn't even make any sense. I hope you see it's wrong.

Social media is used for gossip and keeping up with your fellow man.
It could be used for creating wealth and executing our business plans.

Politicians are politicking, gathering votes for upcoming elections.
Hoping that we'll see the smokescreen instead of deeply reflecting

What happened to our self-love? What happened to our song?
What happened to the pride we felt all day long?

All the while, we sit quietly unbothered, distracted by the whistles and bells
Waking up each day to poverty and dirt packed under our nails.

Daily Inspirations

At the beginning of 2021, I began creating and posting daily inspirations on my social media pages. I plan to compile them at the end of the year to create a daily inspirations book. My inspirations are written each morning between 6:00 a.m. – 7:00 a.m. I actually sit and wait for the words to come before I get ready for my day. Whatever pops up in my spirit is what I type, so there's no particular order or reasoning for the subject of the inspiration. I want to include a few in this book.

> **Are you a negative thinker?**

Ever wonder why some people only search for negative information? Every wonder why they can't look for the positives? **Is this you?**

If so, then it's time for you to do some deep soul searching. Ask God to help you see what's the root cause of this pattern. It's in your heart. Ask God to free you of your negative mindset. It's an ugly disease. Positive change begins in the mind.

"If you change the way you look at things, the things you look at change." -Wayne Dyer

MARY BROWN
DAILY INSPIRATION

"Finally, brothers, whatever is true, whatever is honorable, whatever is just, whatever is pure, whatever is lovely, whatever is commendable, if there is any excellence, if there is anything worthy of praise, think about these things. " Philippians 4:8 ESV

Dark Emotions

Why Not You?

You are always rooting for others. You help them chase their dreams. They call on you to help them accomplish their goals.

You cook, clean, visit, and make yourself available for everyone. Who does these things for you? If it's good enough for them, then why not you?

If starting a business, publishing a book, getting a new car, buying a home, going back to school, running for public office, taking a vacation, getting married, changing your career, etc. is good enough for them, then WHY NOT YOU?

— **MARY BROWN**
DAILY INSPIRATION

And Jesus said to him, "'If you can'! All things are possible for one who believes." Mark *9:23 ESV*

It's okay to walk alone!

You don't need to seek everyone's approval. All company isn't good company. There's no need to follow the crowd. Be who God has called you to be. A benefit of walking alone is you don't have to wonder whether someone else will run off and leave you. You don't have to slow down and wait for someone to catch up with your pace. Don't sacrifice your goals waiting on the approval and company of others. Go alone, even if you have to go afraid.

— **MARY BROWN**
DAILY INSPIRATION

"Be strong and courageous. Do not fear or be in dread of them, for it is the Lord your God who goes with you. He will not leave you or forsake you." Deuteronomy 31:6 ESV

Dark Emotions

Let them talk! Hold your peace!

We all know Jesus didn't do anyone wrong, yet; some people still mistreated and talked badly about him. What do you think that means for us? Let your critics and enemies talk. Just see it as more exposure and free publicity on your behalf. Remember: *"An empty wagon makes a lot of noise."* -Francis Gates

MARY BROWN
DAILY INSPIRATION

"The mouth of a godly person gives wise advice, but the tongue that deceives will be cut off."
Proverbs 10:31 NLT

God wants you to be happy. Put down the excess baggage and live your life.

Why are you carrying everyone else's weights? You're only making their loads lighter. It's time to drop their problems back on their doorsteps. Don't apologize for wanting peace in your life. You have enough worries. Put down the extra baggage. Life is too short! Be happy!

MARY BROWN
DAILY INSPIRATION

"For each one should carry their own load." Galatians 6:5NIV

Black History
Survey Questions & Responses

Although I am not a well-known and prolific researcher, I believe in gathering information to help make a point. I don't need the information to help me prove a point. The points are evident. I just collect and use data to magnify the issues that are already present. I love using data to teach and inform others. This is not a book of scholarly research. It was created to highlight the accomplishments of just a few of the many Blacks who are serving as positive role models.

I created a quick survey using Survey Monkey and asked people to help. The survey was titled "Black History Survey." I placed the link on my personal Facebook page. The survey was made available for one week. I knew that wouldn't be enough time to solicit a lot of participation. I just wanted to receive feedback from the survey I created. I received 56 responses.

As you read the responses, please ask yourself the following questions:
- What are your thoughts?
- What's alarming?
- What's reassuring?
- What else would you like to know?
- How can you use this information to help make your community better?
- How can you use this information to begin additional conversations in your household?

Dark Emotions

Q1 What is your race or ethnicity?

Answered: 56 Skipped: 0

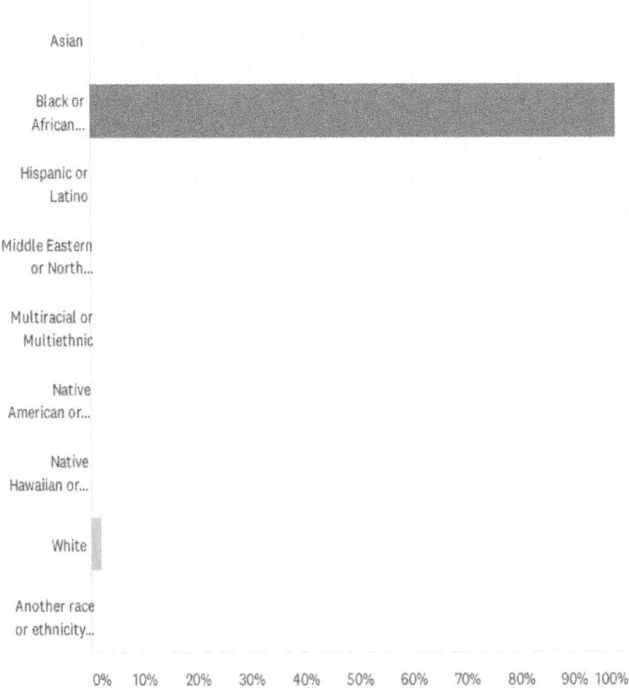

ANSWER CHOICES	RESPONSES	
Asian	0.00%	0
Black or African American	98.21%	55
Hispanic or Latino	0.00%	0
Middle Eastern or North African	0.00%	0
Multiracial or Multiethnic	0.00%	0
Native American or Alaska Native	0.00%	0
Native Hawaiian or other Pacific Islander	0.00%	0
White	1.79%	1
Another race or ethnicity, please describe below	0.00%	0
TOTAL		56

Dark Emotions

Q2 What is the highest level of education you have completed?

Answered: 56 Skipped: 0

BLACK HISTORY SURVEY

ANSWER CHOICES	RESPONSES	
Did not attend school	0.00%	0
1st grade	0.00%	0
2nd grade	0.00%	0
3rd grade	0.00%	0
4th grade	0.00%	0
5th grade	0.00%	0
6th grade	0.00%	0
7th grade	0.00%	0
8th grade	0.00%	0
9th grade	1.79%	1
10th grade	0.00%	0
11th grade	3.57%	2
Graduated from high school	5.36%	3
1 year of college	3.57%	2
2 years of college	10.71%	6
3 years of college	5.36%	3
Graduated from college	17.86%	10
Some graduate school	1.79%	1
Completed graduate school	50.00%	28
TOTAL		56

Dark Emotions

Q3 What is your gender?

Answered: 56 Skipped: 0

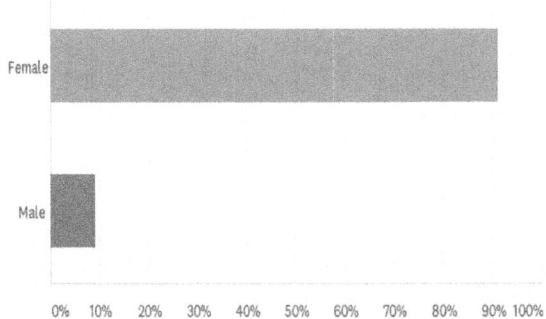

ANSWER CHOICES	RESPONSES	
Female	91.07%	51
Male	8.93%	5
TOTAL		56

Q4 What is your age?

Answered: 56 Skipped: 0

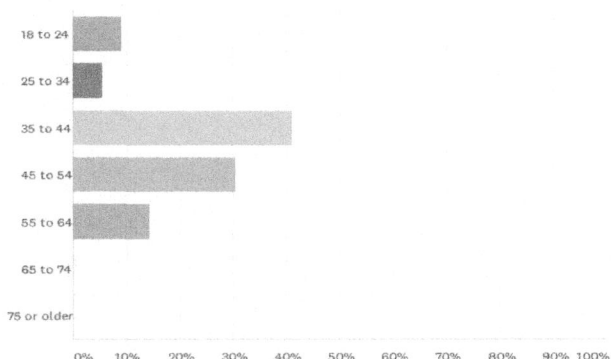

ANSWER CHOICES	RESPONSES	
18 to 24	8.93%	5
25 to 34	5.36%	3
35 to 44	41.07%	23
45 to 54	30.36%	17
55 to 64	14.29%	8
65 to 74	0.00%	0
75 or older	0.00%	0
TOTAL		56

Q5 In what state or U.S. territory do you live?

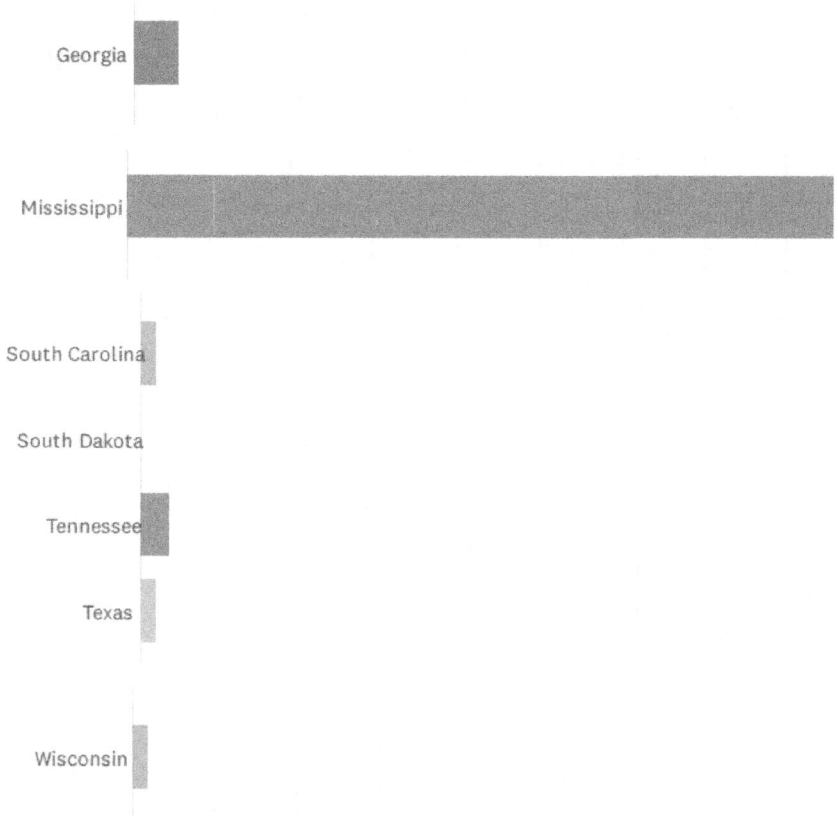

Q6 What is your approximate average household income?

Answered: 56 Skipped: 0

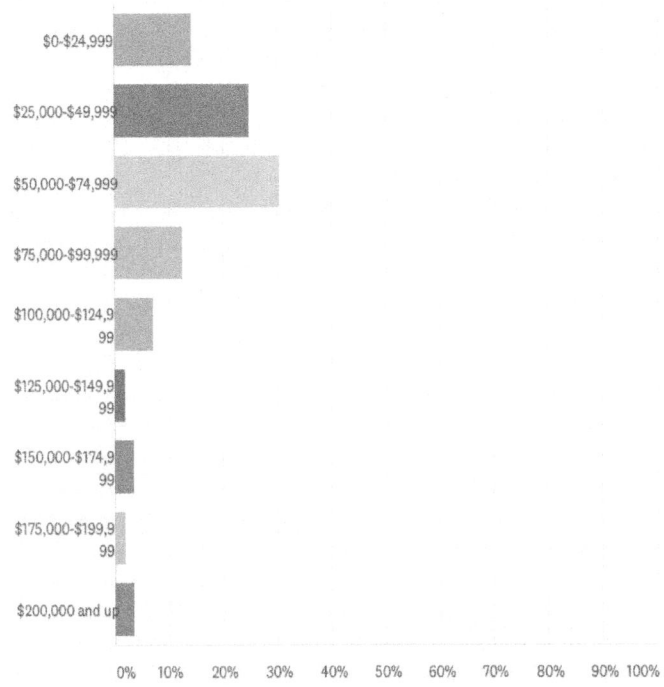

ANSWER CHOICES	RESPONSES	
$0-$24,999	14.29%	8
$25,000-$49,999	25.00%	14
$50,000-$74,999	30.36%	17
$75,000-$99,999	12.50%	7
$100,000-$124,999	7.14%	4
$125,000-$149,999	1.79%	1
$150,000-$174,999	3.57%	2
$175,000-$199,999	1.79%	1
$200,000 and up	3.57%	2
TOTAL		56

Dark Emotions

Q7 How important is attending church to you and your household?

Answered: 56 Skipped: 0

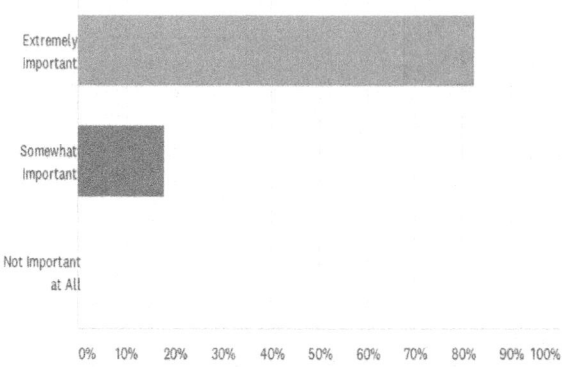

ANSWER CHOICES	RESPONSES	
Extremely Important	82.14%	46
Somewhat Important	17.86%	10
Not Important at All	0.00%	0
TOTAL		56

Q8 How important is Black History to you?

Answered: 56 Skipped: 0

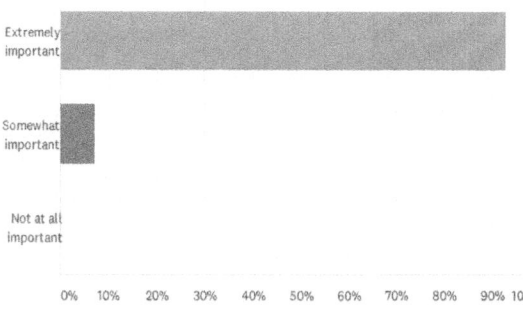

ANSWER CHOICES	RESPONSES	
Extremely important	92.86%	52
Somewhat important	7.14%	4
Not at all important	0.00%	0
TOTAL		56

Dark Emotions

Q9 Should Black History and other African American topics be taught in all grades in schools?

Answered: 56   Skipped: 0

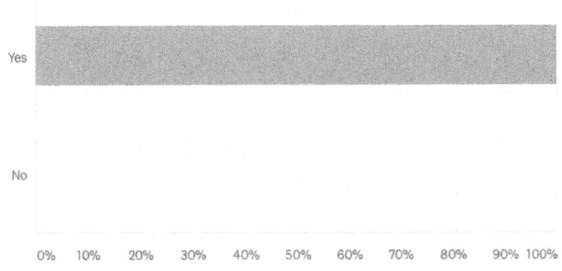

ANSWER CHOICES	RESPONSES	
Yes	100.00%	56
No	0.00%	0
TOTAL		56

Q10 How often is Black History discussed in your home?

Answered: 56   Skipped: 0

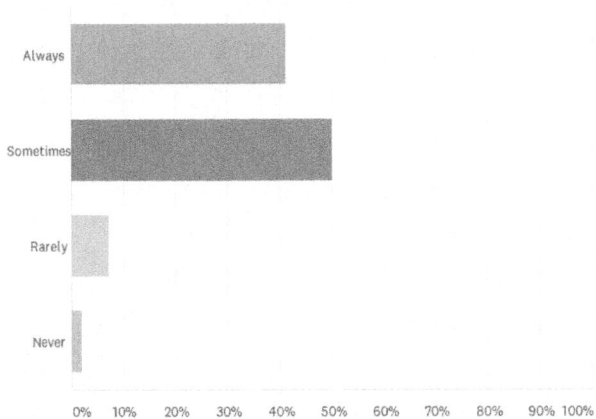

ANSWER CHOICES	RESPONSES	
Always	41.07%	23
Sometimes	50.00%	28
Rarely	7.14%	4
Never	1.79%	1
TOTAL		56

Q11 How supportive are Blacks of Black leadership in your community?

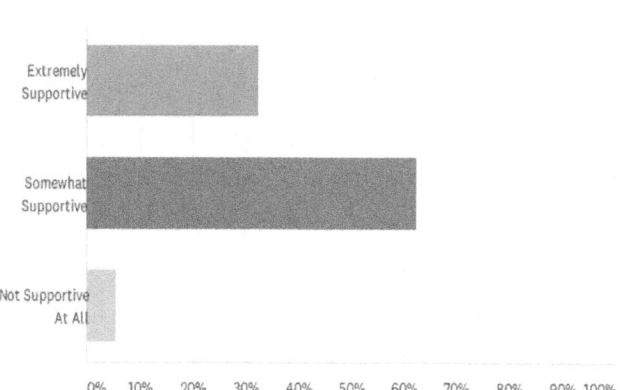

ANSWER CHOICES	RESPONSES	
Extremely Supportive	32.14%	18
Somewhat Supportive	62.50%	35
Not Supportive At All	5.36%	3
TOTAL		56

Dark Emotions

Q12 How would you compare the protests of Mr. George Floyd in 2020, to the Civil Rights marches in the 1960s?

Answered: 56   Skipped: 0

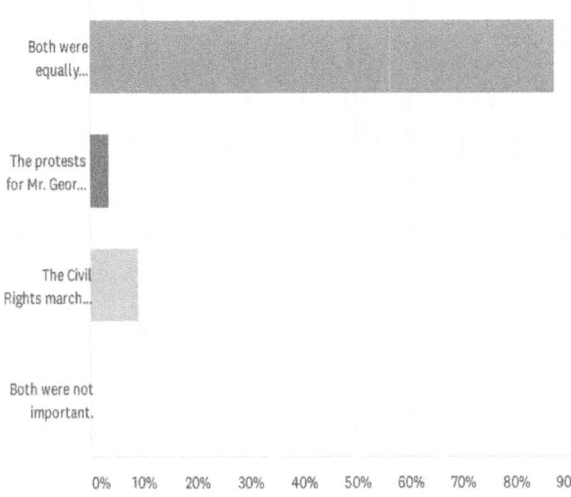

ANSWER CHOICES	RESPONSES	
Both were equally important.	87.50%	49
The protests for Mr. George Floyd were more important.	3.57%	2
The Civil Rights marches were more important.	8.93%	5
Both were not important.	0.00%	0
TOTAL		56

Dark Emotions

Q13 Given the history of mistreatment of Blacks by the police and criminal justice system, how much do you trust law enforcement?

Answered: 56 Skipped: 0

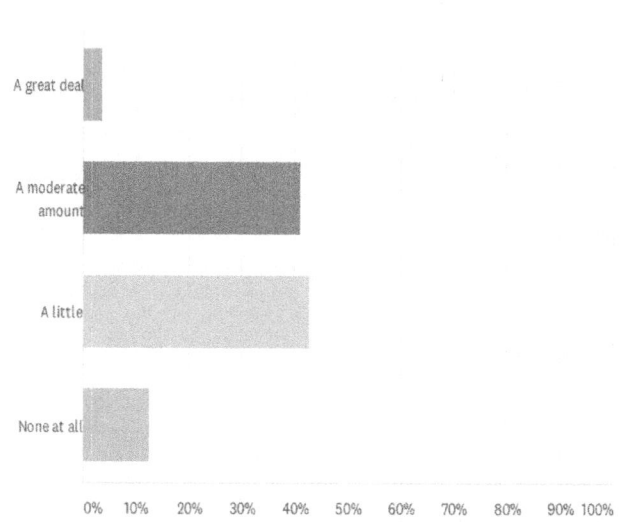

ANSWER CHOICES	RESPONSES	
A great deal	3.57%	2
A moderate amount	41.07%	23
A little	42.86%	24
None at all	12.50%	7
TOTAL		56

Q14 Have you experienced any racial discrimination?

Answered: 56 Skipped: 0

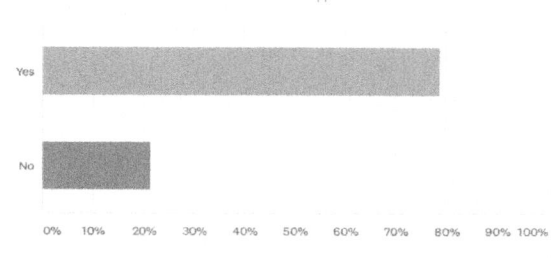

ANSWER CHOICES	RESPONSES	
Yes	78.57%	44
No	21.43%	12
TOTAL		56

Dark Emotions

Q15 Have you experienced racial discrimination as it relates to career advancement?

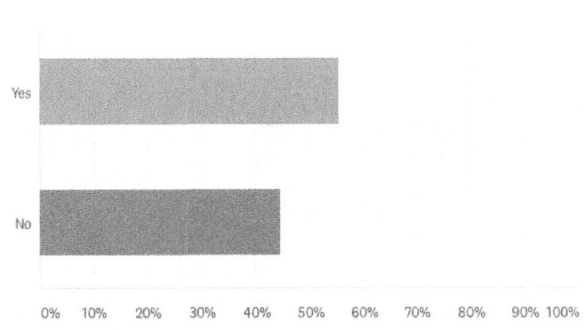

ANSWER CHOICES	RESPONSES	
Yes	55.36%	31
No	44.64%	25
TOTAL		56

Q16 In your job field, are there wage disparities (differences in pay) among blacks and whites?

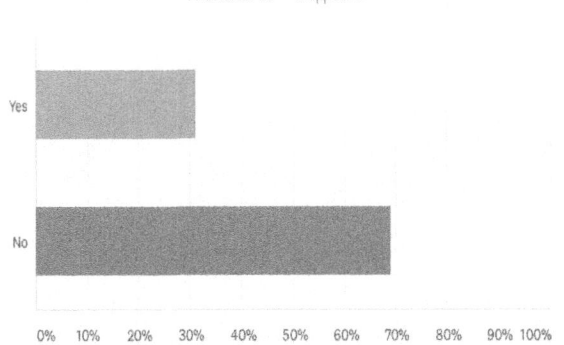

ANSWER CHOICES	RESPONSES	
Yes	30.91%	17
No	69.09%	38
TOTAL		55

Dark Emotions

Q17 How satisfied are you by the way Black men are portrayed in movies?

Answered: 56   Skipped: 0

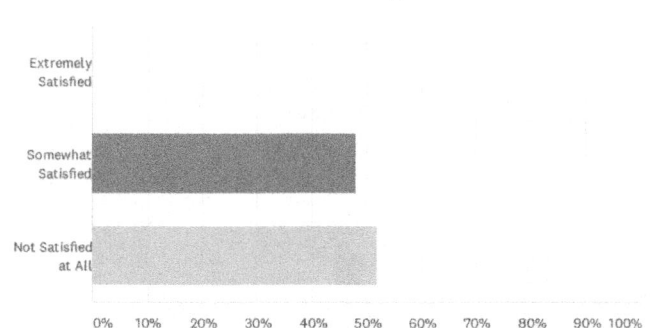

ANSWER CHOICES	RESPONSES	
Extremely Satisfied	0.00%	0
Somewhat Satisfied	48.21%	27
Not Satisfied at All	51.79%	29
TOTAL		56

Q18 How satisfied are you with the way Black men are portrayed in the news/media?

Answered: 56   Skipped: 0

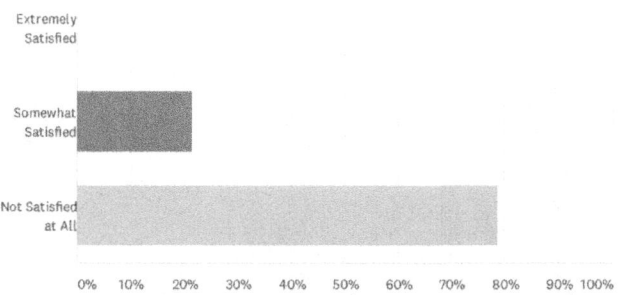

ANSWER CHOICES	RESPONSES	
Extremely Satisfied	0.00%	0
Somewhat Satisfied	21.43%	12
Not Satisfied at All	78.57%	44
TOTAL		56

Dark Emotions

Q19 How satisfied are you with the way Black women are portrayed in movies/media?

Answered: 56   Skipped: 0

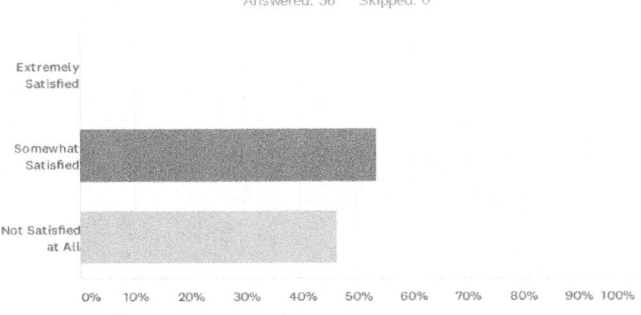

ANSWER CHOICES	RESPONSES	
Extremely Satisfied	0.00%	0
Somewhat Satisfied	53.57%	30
Not Satisfied at All	46.43%	26
TOTAL		56

Q20 How did the law enforcement's response to the storming of the Capitol Building on January 6, 2021, compare to their response to the Black Lives Matter (BLM) protests?

Answered: 56   Skipped: 0

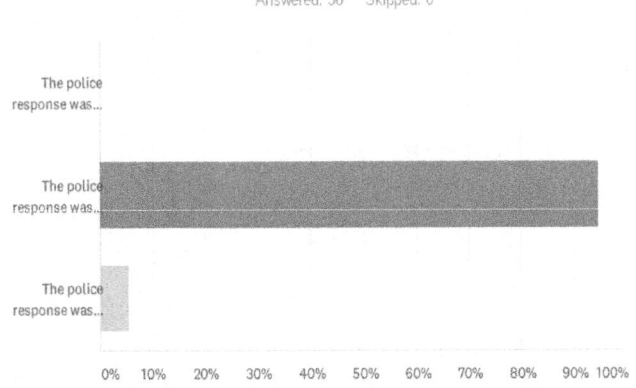

ANSWER CHOICES	RESPONSES	
The police response was the same.	0.00%	0
The police response was more aggressive with BLM protestors than the Capitol Building rioters.	94.64%	53
The police response was more aggressive with the Capitol Building rioters than the BLM protestors.	5.36%	3
TOTAL		56

Dark Emotions

Q21 Have race-relations between Blacks and Whites improved in your community?

Answered: 56   Skipped: 0

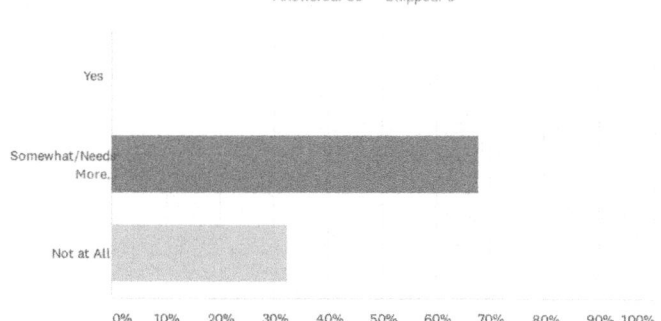

ANSWER CHOICES	RESPONSES	
Yes	0.00%	0
Somewhat/Needs More Improvement	67.86%	38
Not at All	32.14%	18
TOTAL		56

Q22 How supportive are Black people of Black-owned businesses in your community?

Answered: 56   Skipped: 0

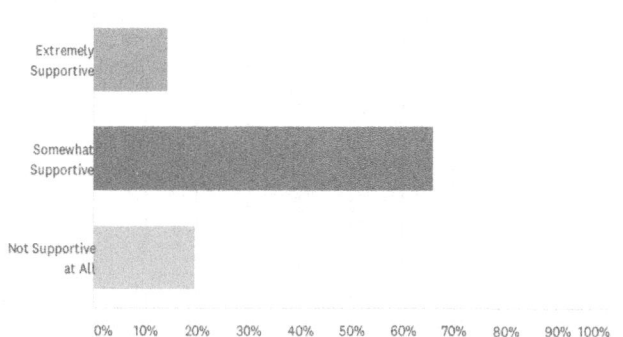

ANSWER CHOICES	RESPONSES	
Extremely Supportive	14.29%	8
Somewhat Supportive	66.07%	37
Not Supportive at All	19.64%	11
TOTAL		56

144

Dark Emotions

Q23 How supportive are Non-Blacks of Black-owned businesses in your community?

Answered: 56   Skipped: 0

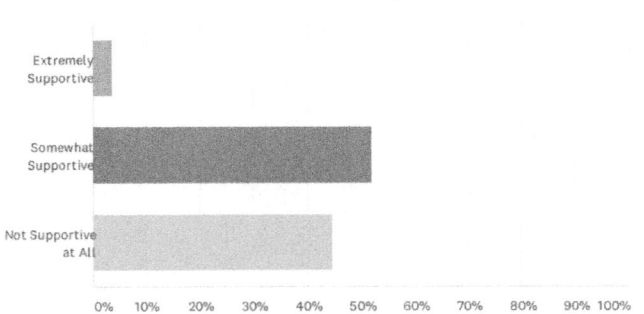

ANSWER CHOICES	RESPONSES	
Extremely Supportive	3.57%	2
Somewhat Supportive	51.79%	29
Not Supportive at All	44.64%	25
TOTAL		56

Q24 Do you believe healthcare disadvantages towards the Black community are a factor in the overall death rate of Black people in the United States?

Answered: 56   Skipped: 0

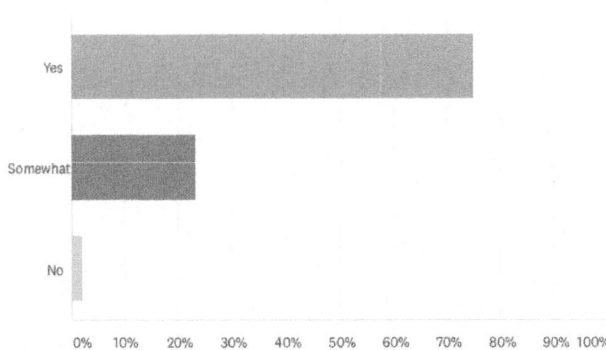

ANSWER CHOICES	RESPONSES	
Yes	75.00%	42
Somewhat	23.21%	13
No	1.79%	1
TOTAL		56

Dark Emotions

Q25 Do you believe healthcare disadvantages towards the Black community are a factor in the COVID-19 death rates of Black people in the United States?

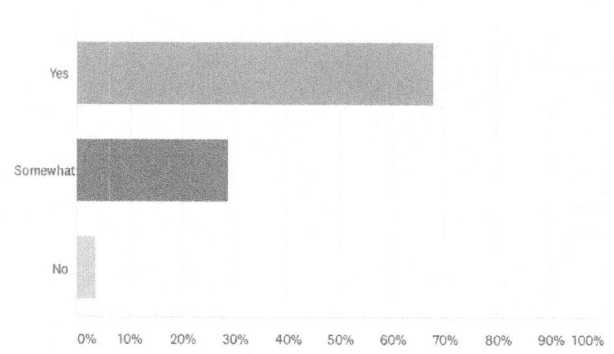

ANSWER CHOICES	RESPONSES	
Yes	67.86%	38
Somewhat	28.57%	16
No	3.57%	2
TOTAL		56

Dark Emotions

Q26 What advice would you give to Black men raising sons in 2021?

Answered: 55   Skipped: 1

Word Cloud: These are the most commonly used words from the responses.

take home make sure need black families life active raising respect positive father Teach young sons present love educated lives show role model child life children important Pray stay church

These are the open-ended responses to question #26:

1. Marry the mother of your children and have a solid family unit.
2. Be transparent
3. Pray and have faith
4. Don't raise your sons in Mississippi.
5. Teach your sons by modeling.
6. Spend quality time with your sons.
7. Support them through your presence, positive examples, and prayers.
8. Teach them and protect them.
9. Always put God first in all you do. Be honest and realistic about the ways of this world, and make sure he knows his history so he will in turn know his trajectory.
10. Pray
11. Be a role model for your sons and show them the right way.
12. Teach him the true value of love and a dollar. Teach him that pride will only teach him a hard lesson.
13. Teach him how to handle rejection.
14. Stay prayed up.
15. Be active role models in their lives.
16. Teach them to love themselves. Be thankful. Keep God first. Make great choices.

17. Teach them the value of being educated. Teach them what it looks like to be racially profiled and how to peacefully save their lives.
18. Fear God and raise your own sons.
19. Be an active participant in your children's lives, especially your sons. Teach them how to be smart, educated with morals and values.
20. Raise your child not to fear anyone but God and that everyone is equal. He is never beneath anyone or race.
21. Be available and visible.
22. Be a positive influence in their lives. Teach them to respect themselves as well as others. Teach them about our Lord and Savior.
23. Please try to abide by the laws so that they can come home safe to their families each night!
24. Be present in your child's life.
25. Be strong and firm with them. Educate them.
26. Be supportive as well as a role model.
27. Teach them respect, integrity, the importance of education, being appreciative, and to know God, which is the most important thing.
28. Pray
29. Show me your friends and I will show you your future.
30. Train them.
31. Be there for your sons.
32. Be more involved in their lives.
33. Make sure you step up to the plate and be a better father figure to your son and any young Black man in your life. This will help shape and mold them into great individuals.
34. In 2021, make sure you are involved in their lives. You need to be a positive role model for your child.
35. Be very supportive of your sons.
36. Put God first. Model the way. Teach your sons how to be real men by living a life that speaks louder than your words.
37. Be a role model. Encourage them to be great. Direct your sons toward the word of God.
38. Teach them about Black History.

39. Blacks need to come forward and raise their sons. It takes a village to raise children. Our young men need their fathers to stand up and be fathers. I'm speaking of those who are not.
40. Be a positive role model from the beginning. Treat their mothers with respect regardless of the relationship situation and treat all women with respect. At a young age, teach your sons that they are somebody. Most importantly, teach them to love God and obey his commandments. And, don't just send them to church; take them to church- with you.
41. Educate them.
42. Be vigilant in training.
43. Be active in their lives 100%.
44. If you are a black man raising a son, please stay present in their lives and home. Not only should you stay present, but take the leadership handle with love and humility. Do not be abusive any factor of life, yet embrace God with all that you have inside and out. Find the right churches, through prayer and supplication, to take your families to at all times. Be a positive, honest light filled with integrity in your community, church, and home. Keep a job. Read your Bibles with your families. Love, love, and continue to love.
45. Teach your sons about the two different US.
46. Teach them how to lead and make sure they get an education.
47. Stay in your son's life. Teach him how to be a man not a boy or somebody's N-word (Black or White). Teach him regardless of the color of his skin that he can raise above anything he puts his mind to.
48. Teach them how to love themselves.
49. Don't sugarcoat anything. Have open and upfront conversations about everything. Be a positive role model for your son.

50. It's important to be present as a parent, especially to your black sons because that plays a major part in the child's life. A non-present father could have the son looking in the streets for love so my advice would just be to show that young man that he doesn't have to be in the streets to feel accepted.

51. Be an example for your sons because they see what you do.
52. Be positive and stay involved. Keep your son active in positive things.
53. Teach him about life.
54. Be present.

Dark Emotions

Q27 What advice would you give to Black women raising daughters in 2021?

Answered: 55 Skipped: 1

Word Cloud: These are the most commonly used words from the responses.

watching first young ladies way women raising daughters men positive gave God education love lives Teach never daughter things know best Pray show black women raising Teach respect

These are the open-ended responses to question #27:
1. Respect themselves.
2. Be transparent.
3. Pray and have faith
4. Train her to be a very responsible achiever with morals.
5. Be an example.
6. Teach them how to respect themselves.
7. Support them by being present, positive examples, and praying daily.
8. Protect your family.
9. Protect your family.
10. Pray for and with her. Love her and make sure she understands how to put herself first when necessary. Let her know that God for her is truly more than a world against her and let her know, being Black is not a reason to be apologetic.
11. Pray
12. Be a role model for your daughters and show them the right way.
13. Love yourself before anybody else does.
14. Tell them you love them more often.

Dark Emotions

15. Stay prayed up. Be better role models. Put God first.
16. Teach them to be young girls.
17. Be true to who you are. Be honest. Treat people right.
18. They need to understand police brutality about black men and some things they can do save their sons, spouses, or male relatives. They need to also be advised of competition and jealousy of women in the same ethnicity and others as well.

19. Fear God and rear your daughters.
20. The advice I would black women raising daughters are exemplify positive role models, be respectful to self and others. Set boundaries and structure in the home.
21. Same advice I gave the men, but never let anyone hurt you the wrong spot, pressure you into doing anything you don't want to do, never let anyone talk down to you and you be whatever you want to be same got for black boys

22. Lead by example
23. Teach them how to respect themselves and how to be classy young women. Promote education and teach them how to defend their themselves against racism and prejudice issues

24. Teach them to value themselves so that they won't be taken advantage of then someone else cheers them on.
25. Teach them to love themselves how they are.
26. Encourage and support them. Show them how to be strong and independent.
27. Be willing to listen but show your daughter that you are mother before a friend.
28. Teach them how to respect themselves pray for wisdom and knowledge. Have integrity, get an education, love yourself. Stay focus and through God all things are possible

29. Make them love themselves and know they don't have to be naked or disrespect their bodies to find love.
30. Let's work together to promote each other.
31. Train them.
32. Raise your daughters the right way.
33. Be more involved in their lives.
34. Be mindful of the things you do in front of your daughter because they are watching. Never let them go freely always be accountable.
35. My advice for black women raising daughters in 2021 would be to encourage and motivate your daughter to do their best. Let your daughter know she is beautiful and be a mother instead of trying to be her friend. Lastly, watch the men you bring around your daughter.

36. Be very supportive of your daughters.
37. Model the Way. Children learn what they see. Tell your daughters that they are beautiful daily. Build their self-esteem at home. Teach them to value themselves. Always lead them to Christ!
38. Model the Way. Children learn what they see. Tell your daughters that they are beautiful daily. Build their self-esteem at home. Teach them to value themselves. Always lead them to Christ!
39. Be a great role model, teach our young ladies to be little ladies, get their education. First for most teach them about the word of God

40. Teach them about Black History.
41. Mothers be firm and Consistence and raising your daughters to be young ladies Consistence and raising your daughters to be young ladies
42. Teach them to love God and honor his commandments. Teach them to honor their bodies; it is a temple, and that making mistakes don't define them. Teach them that is

order to love someone, they must first love themselves. The best advice my mom gave me and I would give to black women raising daughters in 2021- I'm your mother, not your friend!

43. Educate them.
44. Be vigilant and honest.
45. Teach them how to be respectable and productive, self-independent, and God-fearing ladies.
46. If you are a black woman raising a daughter, please be present in the child's/children's lives. Please be a positive driving force willing to take charge if you have to. Impart wisdom in your daughters, not only speaking it, but living it. Try to keep them out of harm's way. Use the Bible to reinforce yours and their way of living. Clothe your temples with righteousness. Never degrade them. Love them with all you have. Be compassionate. Always exhibit the "Fruit of the Spirit" found in God's Holy Bible.
47. Don't give up
48. Raise them to be strong and independent and make sure they get a good education.
49. Show her how to be a woman. Let her know she's just as equal to a man. She can do whatever it is she needs to do with and without a man. Teach her she's beautiful in her own skin. Her hair is prefect the way it is. Teach her she's born royal already!!
50. Teach them how to love and respect themselves and that they are important.
51. Same advice as number 50.
52. Lead her in the right direction. Basically, just lead by example.
53. Watch what you do because they are watching you. Talk to them more.
54. Be positive and keep busy with positive things.

55. Teach them about men and how to act as women.
56. Hold them accountable.

Dark Emotions

Q28 What advice would you give to Black students (ages 0-21) regarding their education?

Answered: 55 Skipped: 1

Word Cloud: These are the most commonly used words from the responses.

Learn Reach tell much use Always future Keep God first take advice Stay school need best Never education degree give Education key success important black students strive Remember will Keep everything hard Please

These are the open-ended responses to question #28:
1. Stay in school and strive hard to reach your dreams.
2. Get the best education afforded to you.
3. Keep God first.
4. My advice would be to get a much if an education as you would like. A four-year degree doesn't mean you're better than the man with the associate degree or certificate in a chosen field.
5. Do your best and add change to it.
6. Education is the key to success.
7. Strive for greatness in everything they do.
8. Get a good education however long it takes.
9. Keep God first and do the best you can. Never use the words "I can't do it."
10. Education is a tool every Black person needs to have in their arsenal. To get ahead is to Love the Lord, heed His word and USE your head=Get an education.
11. Pray
12. Do your very best to complete high school or get a GED so that you can have a stepping stone for life after that.

13. Education is something that no one can take from you and it can take to unimaginable heights. Keep God first and remember that consistency is the key.

14. Always try to be the best at anything that you do.
15. Never underestimate the power of an education. Learn all that you can and know when to apply it.
16. Reach for the stars. Set goals and work toward them.
17. Stay in school. Get your education. It will take you far.
18. Stay humble but focused. Make it a priority and do everything they can to finish.
19. Please get an education and be supportive of your community.
20. The advice I will give is to tell black students how important education is and to strive to be the best. Plan for higher education for success in the future.

21. Be your best and stop students every class and everything. Don't let anyone tell you what you cannot do.
22. They sky is the limit.
23. Get your education while you can.
24. I would tell them to please get an education while it's still possible because you can't tell what the future of education may look like or cost in the future.
25. Remember set your goals and achieve them in your mind first.
26. Education is the key to success.
27. Be willing to explore. Learn as much as possible.
28. Education is very essential and important. Stay in school and stay focused.
29. It is very important to take advantage of all the educational opportunities that are given to you. Use these opportunities to make an easier path for your future.

30. Never stop reading.
31. Keep up the good work.
32. Education is vitally important to your future.

33. Get as much as you can.
34. Remember the sky is the limit. Never use excuses because failure is not an option.
35. My advice to Black students regarding education would be to stay in school and do your best. Do not give up.
36. Stay in school until u complete 12th grade. Go to college and get a degree. Without an education, you will not be become anything in this world.
37. Trust in God for everything you need and don't need. Keep pushing forward. Reach and achieve your goals and dreams.
38. Stay in school, learn all they can. Always pray and seek God; pit God first in everything and all things.
39. Education is very important. Finish high school go to college get you a career
40. I was saying to young black student. Make sure you go to school get a good education stand school. And don't drop out
41. I would give them the same advice my mom gave me- Education is the way out of poverty; education is power when used wisely.
42. Strive to do your best in whatever you do
43. Please get one!
44. Take it seriously. Act as if your life depends on it because it really does.
45. As my father, which is my pastor, always says you can do nothing without Christ and an education. Make sure you get an education while we are still able to. Education is key to your growth as a whole.
46. Education is the key.
47. You need an education to survive.
48. Keep striving. When time gets rough striving a little harder. Never for no reason give up!

49. Education is important and that is something no one can ever take from you.
50. Education is the key to success. Even if you think you are not as smart as you should be, you won't know if you can achieve your goals unless you try.
51. Don't give up. No matter how hard it may seem just don't give up. All the stress will be worth it in the end when you have that degree

52. Please stay in school
53. Take responsibility of your own learning.
54. Watch your friends.
55. Obey your teachers.

Dark Emotions

Q29 What advice would you give to young Black males (ages 0-21) regarding law enforcement in 2021?

Answered: 55 Skipped: 1

Word Cloud: These are the most commonly used words from the responses.

respect police Know Understand live don t trust Follow surroundings rights give law Always respectful life law enforcement careful stay Obey God keep don t

These are the open-ended responses to question #29:
1. Respect the police.
2. Know your rights, and remain calm.
3. Keep God first.
4. There are just certain things a black man should train a black male to do regarding law enforcement. I'd say... contact a reliable parent and follow the rules of the law. Don't talk smart, talk back, or step out of character. Remain calm

5. Follow the law and document and get home early
6. Follow commands to survive.
7. Be careful and always try to pay attention to your surroundings.
8. Respect them regardless. They are waiting for you to act any type of way.
9. Always use common sense. Be obedient to the law and respect it.
10. Be wise. Wisdom is knowing and understanding that your life is more important than any point you can make in the heat of a moment with an overzealous officer/Law Enforcement figure.

11. Pray and get an education.
12. Understand that you must be compliant at all times.
13. An educated Black is like finding a diamond in the rough. It's beautiful when it undergoes pressure.
14. Understand that the law will be looking for any reason to take you out. Don't be the reason.
15. Be respectful and do as you are told.
16. Be conscious of your surroundings and of the people you are around.
17. Treat everyone the same.
18. Record as soon as possible. Obey all commands. Be as honest as possible but don't let your guards down.
19. Respect the law and be obedient to the law. Watch your surroundings.
20. Stay out of trouble and if you are stopped by the police corporate with them no matter how wrong they are until you can get to family to prove your case and get hire a lawyer if necessary.

21. Do as the police say but at the same time don't' let them racial profile you.
22. Follow all instructions with a good attitude.
23. Get your education.
24. I would advise them to be respectful and do what they are asked until they are able to have witnesses to any violation they may be incurring.

25. If you see them immediately get on your phone and call someone.
26. Obey the law but also know your rights.
27. Know your rights. However, don't be so aggressive. Be smart but not smart mouthed. Know the difference.
28. Stay humble and don't provoke them.
29. Remain quiet and respectful.
30. Don't trust anyone.
31. Remember you are Black. That means nothing to some police.

32. Stay out of trouble.
33. Avoid confrontations at any cost.
34. Be very careful.
35. My advice you young black males regarding law enforcement in 2021 is to be respectful. If you pulled over be quiet and do what they ask.

36. Support your community and don't stay in the same position.
37. To always obey the laws of the land, just like God told us to do in the Bible. Vengeance belongs to God. If someone does wrong to you, give it to God and watch Him fight your battles for you. It may not be easy but you have to do it. Your life depends on you trusting God to cover and protect you in all situations.

38. Listen, do what they say. They have control. Unfortunately, at that time, your life is in their hands.
39. Always try to do right and stay out of the lawman's way. Don't' trust any of them.
40. I was sent to young black stew when stopped by the police put your hands up don't talk back listen to what they say so did you don't get shot reaching for your cell phone Just be compliant with the officer do what they tell you to do if you have a sale phone record what's going on
41. It is sad that in this day and age our young black males fear law enforcement, but that is the reality of the times we live in. The advice I gave my sons and would give to others is to respect law enforcement BUT know the law! Educate yourself on your rights as a law-abiding citizen; don't be confrontational- live to fight another day- through the judicial process

42. Be sure to follow the law. Be aware of your surroundings. Do what is right and follow all directives.

Dark Emotions

43. Be respectful. Keep your hands visible. Do all you can to live another day.
44. Just do as they ask so that you may live to go home.
45. Black males, please carry yourselves with respect. Always pray about all situations when encountered by any law enforcement. You must keep a respectful, honorable stance about yourselves. You will know how to do this through constant covering of reading and living as God commands us in His Holy Word.
46. Record everything and just be aware of how they see you.
47. Being Black men, you just need to comply when it comes to law enforcement.
48. Be careful. It's a sad would we live in but always be polite and make few sudden movements. Always have a recorder.
49. Know your rights but also know life isn't fair so stay calm so that you can continue on your journey.
50. Not all law enforcement officers are bad. Learn the law and abide by it. If it's discriminative, do your best the right way to change it.
51. Don't try to act tough with them. Just stay respectful and cooperate.
52. Try to not give the police any reason to harm you.
53. Follow the law and stay positive.
54. Know your purpose.
55. Be careful and don't trust them.

Dark Emotions

Q30 How did you feel when Mrs. Kamala Harris became the First Black Vice President of the United States? Explain.

Answered: 54 Skipped: 2

Word Cloud: These are the most commonly used words from the responses.

respect police **Know** Understand live don t trust **Follow** surroundings **rights** give **law** Always **respectful** life **law enforcement** careful **stay** Obey God keep don t

These are the open-ended responses to question #30:
1. Scared for our country.
2. Overjoyed
3. Mixed emotions
4. Emotional
5. I was proud to see history in the making during our lifetime.
6. Excited, proud, and grateful.
7. Thrilled. It's due time Black women are respected in the workforce.
8. Peacock proud. It was a true honor to witness this with my 37-year-old daughter and my beautiful 7-year-old granddaughter. It shows that hard work, great educational background and determination can and will make your life great.
9. Proud moment
10. Proud
11. I was excited to witness this moment in history.
12. Extremely excited. Let hope heal the land!
13. It was about time it happened.
14. I love it! Women now have a voice. We are no longer unheard.

15. Words cannot explain the impact of just being the first Black VP. She will have an impact on young Black girls and women.
16. I felt amazing. We can do whatever we put our minds to
17. I was overjoyed. It was similar to that of Barack Obama but it was much more personal. It became the example for you can do whatever you want and be whatever you want to be.
18. I thank God for allowing me to witness the day and I said Free at Last Thank God Our young black girls can Have A Dream

19. Very happy.
20. Proud and happy. Women can do whatever men can do.
21. I felt elevated and proud.
22. Great
23. I was very proud to witness this historical occasion!
24. Loved it! Women must win as well!
25. Love it!
26. Very proud and excited.
27. I was overly excited and to God to be the glory. It's been a long time coming, but it happened.
28. I was very elated.
29. Proud
30. Okay!!!
31. I am very excited and honored by this historic honor.
32. Very excited.
33. It made me realize I can be anything I want to be.
34. I felt it was a blessing that the Lord allowed the people of the United States to vote for Mrs. Kamala Harris to serve as the first Black Vice President.
35. Very proud. I am a woman with standards. We as women are very powerful and intelligence individuals with morals and values. I am so proud of kamala Harris as a Black Female.
36. I felt great. A sense of relief, appreciation came over me and gratefulness to God for allowing me to witness such a

historic moment with my own eyes. Other black girls can truly believe that they can do whatever they set their minds to do. God is doing amazing things. God gets all the glory!
37. She a great role model for all female young and old. She will do great; blessings are on her she will go very far.

38. Happy
39. I was very proud and very happy.
40. With the exception of Barack Obama being elected president, it was the happiest I've been in a long time as an African American, as a woman and as a citizen.

41. Great!
42. Great!
43. Overjoyed!
44. I was remarkably moved to see how God allowed a woman of color to be elected as the Vice President of the United States. I felt an overcoming splurge of happenstance. I am very happy to see history being made in my lifetime. It also allows me to see what God can do for anyone who receives Him and a proper education.

45. Awesome!
46. It feels good to know that a black woman can achieve and accomplish anything
47. Happy. It's amazing to see not just a black vice president but a woman. We live to see this day. Our women have to fight ten times harder for anything, so it's a great feeling
48. That the hard work of my African American people was not in vain.
49. Excited....it's another step to showing boys and girls in our community it's possible to become whatever your heart desires. Breaking barriers should be your goal.
50. I was proud mainly because I love to see when black people get in better positions. I love to see everyone

succeed but it's a different type of feeling mg when a black person, especially a black woman, succeed

51. Really happy for her.
52. Overwhelmed with joy. It was a win for all women.
53. It was a great move for Black people.
54. Overjoyed.

After reading the responses, please ask yourself the following questions:
- What are your thoughts?
- What's alarming?
- What's reassuring?
- What else would you like to know?
- How can you use this information to help make your community better?
- How can you use this information to begin additional conversations in your household?

ABOUT THE AUTHOR

MARY MCBRIDE-BROWN was born in the Mississippi Delta in 1977. She is the daughter of the late Mr. Lem Nash and Mrs. Cassandra Nash. She is the mother of Regis, Jr. and Lem.

Mary received her Bachelor of Science degree in Elementary Education from Mississippi Valley State University, located in Itta Bena, MS, in 2002. She returned to MVSU, where she earned a Master's degree in Elementary Education in 2004. She earned her an additional Master's degree in Educational Leadership from Delta State University, in Cleveland, MS, in 2008. She earned a Ph.D. in Educational Leadership from The University of Mississippi, located in Oxford, MS, in 2018.
She is the author of:
Worth of My Words
Worth of My Words: Enormous Power in the Placement of Poems
Dark Emotions: The Mental Cost of Caring About Black Men
Ordained to Suffer: Running from the Bulls, A Memoir
Dark Emotions: Colorful Conversations for Black Women and Girls
Dark Emotions: Alarmed Yet Unbothered in the Mississippi Delta
Dark Emotions; Honoring History Creating Legacy

Email: Brownsound888@gmail.com
Instagram: https://www.Instagram.com/marymbrown77
Twitter: https://www.twitter.com/DrMaryBrown77

Dark Emotions

Made in United States
Orlando, FL
19 February 2024

43871882R10095